Sounding the Mind of God

Therapeutic Sound for
Self-healing and Transformation

First published by O Books, 2009
O Books is an imprint of John Hunt Publishing Ltd., The Bothy, Deershot Lodge, Park Lane, Ropley,
Hants, SO24 0BE, UK
office1@o-books.net
www.o-books.net

Distribution in:

UK and Europe
Orca Book Services
orders@orcabookservices.co.uk
Tel: 01202 665432 Fax: 01202 666219
Int. code (44)

USA and Canada
NBN
custserv@nbnbooks.com
Tel: 1 800 462 6420 Fax: 1 800 338 4550

Australia and New Zealand
Brumby Books
sales@brumbybooks.com.au
Tel: 61 3 9761 5535 Fax: 61 3 9761 7095

Far East (offices in Singapore, Thailand,
Hong Kong, Taiwan)
Pansing Distribution Pte Ltd
kemal@pansing.com
Tel: 65 6319 9939 Fax: 65 6462 5761

South Africa
Stephan Phillips (pty) Ltd
Email: orders@stephanphillips.com
Tel: 27 21 4489839 Telefax: 27 21 4479879

Text copyright Lyz Cooper 2008

Design: Stuart Davies

ISBN: 978 1 84694 211 2

A CIP catalogue record for this book is available
from the British Library.

Printed by CPI Antony Rowe, Chippenham, UK

O Books operates a distinctive and ethical publishing philosophy in
all areas of its business, from its global network of authors to
production and worldwide distribution.

Sounding the Mind of God

Therapeutic Sound for
Self-healing and Transformation

Lyz Cooper

BOOKS

Winchester, UK
Washington, USA

CONTENTS

Introduction   1

Part 1 – Aligning to the Mind of God

The Mind of God   7
Living in Resonance   13
Radiators, Drains and the Universal Breath   19
The Auric Field   24
Energetic Blueprints, Consciousness and Intention   27
Personal Filters and Energetic Roundabouts   35
What We Believe and Why   43
The Human Antenna Array   50
The En-lightenment Process and the Garden of Eden   53
Tribal Patterning and The Ego   60
Youthing, Loving, Age-ing and Sage-ing   64
The Human Brain   67
The Law of the Octave   71
Chakras and Nadis   75
Sacred Listening   95
The Sound of Silence   97
The Breath of Life   101

Part 2 – Sounding the Mind of God

Introduction   111
Wave Patterns and the Particles of Love and Hate   112
Your Sacred Voice   115
Humming   123
Toning   124
Sacred Vowels   127
Working With Your Divine Heart   135
Overtones – Creating a Sonic Rainbow   139
Himalayan Singing Bowls   147

Crystal Bowls   161
The Rhythm of Life   171
Planet Earth Calling – Grounding   187
Full Circle   189
An Invitation   191
Sources   192

*'The mind of God is cosmic music
resonating throughout hyperspace'*

Michio Kaku

Dedication

Happy Birthday Dad

Acknowledgments

To my husband Paul, thank you for your support and for being a good ear when I needed a sounding board; you are also a great grounding influence in my life. Mum, thank you for your help, patience and support over the years. To Michael Endacott (although you are no longer on this plane, I know you can hear me!) and Clive Teal of the Institute for Complementary and Natural Medicine, thank you for helping me to create the first registered sound therapy school in the UK. Clive, thank you for your continued support and guidance. Lianne Fagon, Clifford Sax and Suzanne Inayat Khan, thank you for repeating the "write a book" mantra to me, it worked! Suzanne, thank you for sharing the teachings of Hazrat Inayat Khan with me, I feel truly blessed. Clifford and Fiona, thank you for pulling out the stops at short notice and for producing the graphics – much appreciated!

Jonathan Goldman, Fred Alan Wolf Ph.D, James D'Angelo and Dr Manjir Samanta-Laughton, thank you for your heart-warming comments and wonderful endorsements; your work has been an inspiration to me and I was honored to receive such positive feedback from you. Special thanks to Fred Alan Wolf PhD for your time and extra support with regard to the nature of energy, you helped me to put a missing piece of the jigsaw puzzle into place.

To my friends Judy and Pam, thank you for the positive energy "fixes" and encouragement over the years. A big sonic hug goes to all of the students that have ever trained with the British Academy of Sound Therapy, your sound-work has helped so many people over the years and I love reading all of the amazing testimonials that your clients have written. This is the proof of the wonderful effect that sound has on people's lives, keep up the good work!

Gandiva Lorcan and Surya, you were the first to introduce me to sound and for this I am truly grateful. Even though I did not know at the time I would end up working with sound, I am sure that you facilitated an awakening within me. Heartfelt thanks also go to Anne Nash, your laughter and energy helped me to create my future path in sound.

Thank you to all of the teachers that I have worked with over the years. There are so many to mention so please accept my apologies if I have missed you out. Michael Ormiston, your wonderful tones inspired me to learn overtone singing. Thank you for your teaching and for opening my heart and ears to Khoomii. Rollin Rachelle thank you for introducing me to western style overtoning, you are both true masters. Thank you to Alan Sales for introducing me to the tuning forks and to Daniel Statnekov for making me a wonderful set of Peruvian Whistling Vessels that have been such powerful teachers. Michael Deason-Barrow and Lorin Penny, your wonderful work at Tonalis is very special and I thoroughly enjoyed the time I spent with you. Dr Barry Bittman and Christine Stevens at Healthy Rhythms® your energy, knowledge, experience and love for your work shine through, it was such a pleasure to train with you. Thanks to the Fit Rhythms® gang for sharing your rhythm with me and to Mugenkyo for introducing me to the power and exhilaration of Taiko drumming. Thanks to Nick Heart-Williams for sharing your drum-making knowledge with me. Armi and Sanna, you are wonderful souls, thank you for sharing your drum and Joik with me, my trips to your wonderful country feed my soul. To Jonathan Cope and Paul Wilkinson, you are fonts of information and encouragement as well as a source of wonderful instruments!

Introduction

This is an exciting time to be alive. Advancements in science are helping to support and add a new dimension to thousands of years of spiritual teachings. This synergy is helping to increase the awareness and credibility of holistic therapies, especially in the mainstream. Sound therapy has its roots in ancient practices and, like many holistic therapies, is being rediscovered and further developed to apply to modern living. In this book I will draw from the realms of science and spirituality to explain why sound can be a powerful life-enhancing tool. I will also offer many practical exercises using a variety of different instruments and techniques to help to improve health and wellbeing and for personal transformation.

I was a sensitive child and was aware of the energy beings who occupied other realms. In early adulthood I became interested in holistic health and set out to experience as many different methods as I could. I studied many subjects including shamanism, massage, Reiki and space-clearing and enjoyed working with different self-development techniques, reading books and attending workshops.

In 1991 I approached my local Adult Education Center and began running evening classes in self-development, empowerment, image and confidence building. I loved the teaching-learning process so much that I embarked on a teacher training course which, 18 years later, has led me to the final year of a Master of Arts in Education.

Back to the early 90's. Whilst I was doing my best to feed my soul doing things I loved I still needed to pay the bills, so at the same time as my learning and teaching I was pursuing a career in advertising. I knew that this was not where I wanted to be but I was grateful for the financial reward.

I continued to develop my interest in holistic health and

spiritual development as and when I could, but the workload was increasing in my nine to five job. At the same time I was becoming more and more drawn to working with something that fed my soul. I was also experiencing traumatic relationships in my personal life which I was finding extremely difficult to deal with. Eventually my system caved in under the pressure and I ended up with M.E followed by extreme anxiety and clinical depression. I had been ignoring and resisting my system's call for change for so long that I had manifested dis-ease; it was "pay back time". My physical, emotional and mental levels were in disarray and I didn't know how to get out of the hole I had dug for myself. Eventually I decided that all I could do was surrender completely to the process. I stopped, listened and waited.

Being confined to my bed was the turning point for me. I had no choice but to allow myself the space and time to listen to my heart's desire and advertising featured nowhere in my dream. After being away from work for almost a year I knew I was not going to be able to go back to work again. The very thought of it drained my energy. I took voluntary redundancy and immediately felt an increase in my energy levels. My system was telling me I was on the right track!

I remember a day during my illness when I had a thumping headache. I decided that a bath would be a good idea and whilst in the tub I began toning, enjoying hearing the sound bounce around the walls. Without thinking about it I began to change my pitch, slowly moving up and down the scale, resting on the notes that felt good. After a few minutes I realized that I no longer had my headache! Eureka! (move over Archimedes!). I felt a rush of energy and excitement, had my voice cured my headache? Deep within I knew I was on to something.

I carried on using my voice and found that it was very effective at moving energy around my system. I was so impressed by the speed and effectiveness of such a simple process that I knew I wanted to explore this area further. Shortly after I began working with my voice I found a small metal bowl in a shop and was amazed when this little bowl began to sing its heart out when I ran a stick around the rim! That was my first experience of a singing bowl and it touched something deep inside my heart. I purchased the little bowl and began working with it along with my voice. As my Himalayan bowl collection grew so did my desire to find somewhere to train to be a sound therapist so that I could work with others.

In 1994 contacted the Institute for Complementary and Natural Medicine (ICNM) to find out where I could train, but at that time there were no sound therapy schools in the UK that were registered with any of the membership bodies. I decided to wait for a course to become available and, in the meantime, I continued building a relationship with different instruments, discovering how each sound interacted with the different levels of my being. The sound transported me to realms within and without, increasing my awareness, highlighting imbalances and enabling me to transcend holding patterns. For the first time in my adult life I was able to reach and sustain a deep sense of connectedness and profound inner peace. As a result my outer world changed, my relationships transformed and my health improved.

A year later there was still nowhere to train but I couldn't wait any longer. I had developed a technique that I was really happy with (I also had been working with case studies who had reported very positive results). I presented my work to the ICNM who agreed to give me the support I needed to begin working with others. In 1997 I felt confident in the techniques that I had developed and wanted to share them with others. I formed "Soundworks" and began touring the UK and overseas, sharing my work and gaining further experience and knowledge.

In the year 2000 I formed The British Academy of Sound Therapy (BAST) which became the first school in the UK to offer professional training courses. If I was going to train people to become therapists and practitioners I wanted to offer the highest standard of training and support that was possible so I affiliated my school to as many membership bodies and organizations that I could. I was on a mission to put sound therapy on the map as a powerful way to improve health and wellbeing. Although BAST was the first school in the UK I was certainly not the first sound practitioner. Sound therapy has been used for healing and transformation for thousands of years and there are many wonderful people around the world helping to raise the awareness of this powerful tool.

Just like many other holistic therapies, sound therapy has been forgotten or side-lined in many cultures but there is a buzz out there. It is the sound of this wonderful, powerful and effective therapy being remembered, and it is incredibly exciting!

"Sounding the Mind of God" is a workbook that guides you through a series of exercises using a range of different instruments and techniques. The book is divided into two parts "Aligning to the Mind of God" and "Sounding the Mind of God". Part 1 lays the foundation for the sound-work we will be doing and gives you exercises to identify energy imbalances in the system and enable alignment to take place. Part 2 contains information about how to work with therapeutic sound for personal transformation.

As a result of working with the exercises in this book you may find that your life transforms in the most wonderful ways. This may seem like a bold statement but I have experienced profound change in my life and many people I have worked with have experienced relief from long-term and some times chronic symptoms. It is no accident that you have been drawn to working with sound at this time. If you do not wish to embrace change in your life which is ultimately for the better then I suggest you give this book away now!

Still with me? Wonderful!

Preparation

It is a good idea to keep a journal to record your process and progress as you work through this book. When looking back you may be surprised how much has changed, not only in your life but also in the lives of those around you as the changes that you make will radiate out into your world. Writing your experiences down also helps you to identify patterns that you may not have previously noticed. Rather than diagnosing specific illnesses or conditions you will be assessing your energy system which may point to certain physical, mental or emotional symptoms that you are experiencing in your life.

Everyone has a different reaction to the exercises depending on the imbalances and holding patterns they are working on. If anything comes up that you need help with, seek appropriate support. You do not have to go it alone, nor do you have to push yourself too hard too fast. Be gentle and kind to yourself. Take time to absorb each exercise before moving on to the next and meet your needs accordingly. If you feel stiffness in the body get a massage, join a Tai Chi or Yoga class or do something physical as "stuff" can get stuck in the physical body. If you need support to process something on an emotional or mental level you may choose to see a qualified counselor or psychotherapist. When looking for support there are many good associations and membership bodies that should be able to guide you in the right direction, or ask a friend if they know anyone who can help you. Word of mouth is often the best recommendation.

Therapeutic sound can be used alongside most other complementary therapies as well as orthodox medical treatment, but please consult your GP or other health professional before working with the exercises in this book if you have any concerns. Sound therapy is not intended to replace any medication you are taking or treatment you are receiving. This book is intended to be for self-healing and transformation and does not qualify you to work with others. If you get the calling to be a sound therapist, wonderful! Do your research and find the best professional training course to suit your needs.

All of the exercises in this book require you to be your own personal detective and put yourself in a gentle and loving interrogation room. Resistance is also very common so if there is an exercise that you have resistance to, make a note as this can speak volumes! It may highlight an area that you need to work on. Most importantly enjoy the process. Your experience will be exactly what is right for you at this time. I hope that you will enjoy working with this book as much as I enjoyed writing it and I wish you a happy and enjoyable sound journey!

Part 1 Aligning to the Mind of God

"The mind of God is cosmic music resonating throughout hyperspace"
Michio Kaku

The Mind of God

References to there being a *"universal sound"* appear in almost every culture and spiritual teaching in the world. In India the original sound was called *"nada"*, the primal tone. In Hindu mythology Krishna's flute was the symbol of the sound of creation and the Vedic teachings say that "OM" is the sound of creation of all things. The Bible states, *"in the beginning was the word"* and in the Qur'an the first word was *"fa-yakun"*, meaning *"be!"* and everything came into being. The creation stories of the Australian Aboriginal people speak of a time when there was only one of each species of animal on Earth. Each one of those creatures sang its own song, enabling others of the same species to be created. The Sufis call the primal sound *"Saute Surmad"* which Hazrat Inayat Khan referred to as *"the sound of the manifestation of what is"*. According to Inayat Khan, Muhammad also heard this tone in the sacred caves at Gare Hira. Lao Tzu, the father of Taosim and author of the Tao Te Ching described the Tao as being *"the great tone"*.

Quantum physicists seeking the connection between all things often describe the universe in musical terms. Michio Kaku, dubbed by the *Financial Times* as *"one of the gurus of modern physics"*, describes the universe as a *"symphony of strings"*. In his book *"Parallel Worlds"* he states *"the mind of God is cosmic music resonating throughout hyperspace"*.

From ancient spiritual teachings to cutting edge quantum physics we are reaching the same conclusion, the universe is sound.

Could this be why sound touches us on such a deep level? Most of us at some point in our lives have been deeply moved by a piece of music, whether it is the sound of Gregorian monks chanting in prayer, a soaring piece of Mozart or the first time you heard the Sex Pistols, music has the power to resonate with our deepest and most private emotions, send armies into battle, bring people out of comas, raise the hairs on our arms and move us to tears. However, this book is dedicated to working with *sound*, not music so what is the difference?

Music is sound that has been organized. It is like a sonic cake with each ingredient melting in the ears as the listener explores the layers. In sound therapy we "de-construct" the cake and bring each sound back out of the mix to express itself in its own beautiful, simple way. I believe that it is the interaction between pure sound and the individual that enables profound healing, or "wholing" (a term I prefer to use) to be made. Although music is an extremely powerful force, in my opinion the simplicity of sound allows the system to achieve deeper states of being. Complex melody can influence the brain into staying in a higher frequency because the mind becomes engaged in the music. Both sound therapy and music therapy have a valuable part to play in improving health and wellbeing. They are just different facets of the same wonderful diamond!

Therapeutic sound helps to facilitate the free-flowing of prana (also known as life-force, chi or ki). The uninhibited flow of this universal life energy results in the system balancing itself. Aligning to the mind of God during your wholing sessions creates a connection that allows for change to take place in all areas of your life.

At a fundamental level all objects are made from energy which exists in a state of potential so anything is possible. The resonance of this energy creates a sound which is out of our hearing range, but nevertheless it is there. So from a purely scientific perspective everything in the known universe *is* making a sound. This is the mind of God, the primordial sound that was perceived by Muhammad, Lao Tzu and others.

Your organs, blood, bone and flesh all resonate at different frequencies. As you are reading this book you are emitting a wonderful symphony of sound as individual as your finger-prints. As well as the physical parts of your body you also have mental, emotional and spiritual or etheric parts which will I will refer to as "levels" in this book. The key to working with sound as a therapeutic tool is being able to identify the different levels of being and to determine at what level an imbalance is manifesting. Once you have identified the imbalance you are then able to compose the appropriate "sonic prescription" to help balance the system.

Energetically speaking, the physical level is the densest as it is formed from energy that manifests in the physical form. The emotional level is less dense than the physical level but dense enough to create feelings and emotional responses. The mental level is finer and operates at the level of thought. The etheric or spiritual level is an even finer form of energy and is perhaps the level that is the hardest to identify or define. Some people find the word "spiritual" challenging as it can have connections with religion, but the essence of all religious teachings is about devel-oping a spiritual connection with the divine and all things. The spiritual level is also known as the "energy body" but as every-thing is energy perhaps this is not the most accurate description. For the sake of ease, I will use the word "spiritual" to define this level of being. Later on in this book we will be examining resis-tance, so if you have resistance to the word "spiritual" you may find some of the exercises in this book useful.

Exercise: Identifying the levels of being

Aim: The aim of this exercise is to familiarize yourself with the different levels of your being and identify areas of potential imbalance.

Sit comfortably on a straight-backed chair, put both feet on the floor and bring your attention to the center of your being. Feel the weight of your body on the chair and your feet on the floor.

Tune in to your physical body. Do you feel any pain, discomfort or tension anywhere? Are there physical parts of your body which feel heavy or constricted? Note down where these are and how they feel. Ask your physical body if there is anything that it needs to be free of the discomfort, pain, tension or whatever you are feeling. Don't force an answer; just ask your physical body, listen to what comes up and write it down.

Then move your attention to the emotional level. How do your emotions feel? Are you on a rollercoaster with a mixture of highs and lows or are your emotions stable at the moment? Which emotions are you feeling? If negatively charged emotions such as anger, sadness or fear are present ask your emotional body if there is anything that it needs to be free of these emotions and write down what comes up.

Now move to your mental level. If you were to view your thoughts on a movie screen what would they look like? Would they be calm or racing around? Communicate with your mental body and, as with the other two levels, ask what this level needs right now and note down what comes up.

Finally move to your spiritual level. Can you feel your prana moving through the system? How does it feel? Do you feel tingly, warm, cold or another sensation? Can you feel anything in any of your chakras (if you are unsure about what chakras are you may prefer to turn to the chapter on chakras first and then return to this exercise). Ask your spiritual level if there is anything it needs to enable it to be healthy, strong and free-flowing and note down the answers that you get.

You may find some levels easier to communicate with than others. Note the levels that you find easy and those that you find harder to sense as this could point to areas that need attention. If you find it difficult to communicate with a particular level, ask yourself why this is. If you have difficulty communicating with the physical level could it be because you tend to neglect your physical body for some reason? If this is the case, what can you do to restore balance?

Check in to the levels of your being as often as you can. For optimum health and personal transformation it is ideal to achieve a balance on all levels of being. Asking each level what it needs during your tuning in exercises can produce some very interesting answers and insights. You may be surprised at what comes up! It is also important to be prepared to listen to the answers that you get and make changes accordingly. If your physical level keeps asking you to get a massage and you ignore it don't be surprised if you eventually end up at the osteopath with a huge bill for months of treatment!

Scoring your progress

This scoring system is a useful self-evaluation tool as it provides a snapshot of your current state of being as well as helping you with the tuning in process. It also saves you from having to remember your scores as you can look back to see which areas have improved and which still need work. This self-evaluation tool is similar to the one used by BAST sound therapists and practitioners. By looking back on their clients' scores they can easily see the areas that have improved and those that still need work.

You can scan or photocopy this page and enlarge it if you prefer. You may wish to fill the graph in before and after an exercise, or once a week to record overall progress, whatever suits your needs.

Exercise: Scoring your progress

With one being poor and ten being excellent give each level of being a mark to reflect where you feel you are. Don't think too much about putting the "right" number down, there is no right or wrong, choose the first number that comes to you. When you have marked all of the areas on the graph join them up with a straight line to create a four-sided shape. Depending on your scores it will look more or less like a diamond. The low scores highlight the areas that you may like to give special attention to during your sounding sessions.

The Scoring Diamond

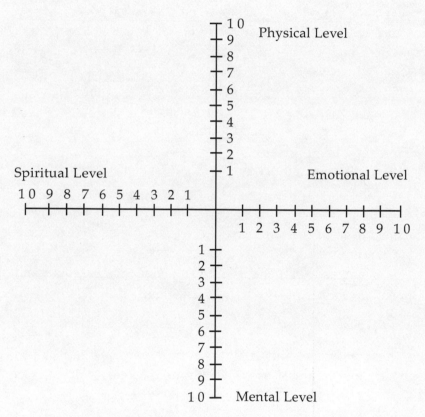

Achieving balance

Sound therapy is an energy medicine. As we are all made from energy at a fundamental level there is no reason why therapeutic sound cannot address any imbalance on any level of being. As the physical level is denser it can sometimes take longer to transmute the energy on the physical level, although this is not always the case. Sometimes people can make quantum shifts, completely clearing their imbalance in one session so anything is possible!

As well as working with sound, give thought to other things you can do to give extra support to the level you are working on. If you have scored low on the physical level what else you can do you can do to support this level of your being? You could do more exercise, get a massage or change your diet, for example. If you gave your spiritual level a low score you could take up meditation or Tai-Chi. The spiritual level can also be nurtured with artwork, pottery, music or gardening, anything that feeds your spirit. All of your levels of being are connected so any changes you make to one level will influence the others to some extent.

"Realigning our frequency is like tuning a string on an instrument to its perfect pitch. The finer the frequencies we emit, the finer the life experience we attract via the universal Law of Resonance".
Jasmuheen

Living in Resonance

We know that everything has a natural resonance. If you were to take a pair of tuning forks of the same frequency, strike one of the forks and hold them fairly close together the un-struck fork will also start to sing. This is because objects of the same or very similar frequency have a mutual influence on each other. This principle is a universal law known as "sympathetic resonance". The Collins English Dictionary describes sympathetic resonance as *"the condition of a body or system when it is subjected to a periodic disturbance of the same frequency as the natural frequency of the body or system. At this frequency the system displays an enhanced oscillation or vibration."*

If strong enough, sympathetic resonance can cause an object to explode or shatter, such as a glass that is smashed by a singer's voice, or a bridge that is brought down by many people marching across it. This is why soldiers break their step when walking over a bridge (the entrainment principle is also present here, which we shall cover later in this chapter).

The walls of Jericho came tumbling down because the sound frequency of the trumpets resonated with the structure of the wall to such an extent that it disintegrated. The same principle is used in modern medicine to treat kidney stones. By matching the frequency of the kidney stone with a laser the atoms within the stone resonate and shatter. In his book *"The Biology of Belief"*, Dr Bruce Lipton states *"there is enough scientific evidence to suspect that we can tailor make a waveform as a therapeutic agent in much the same way as we now modulate chemical structures with drugs."* I believe this is what we are doing when we work with therapeutic sound. We are using sound plus positive focused intention to help the system to rebalance itself.

In *"The Mystery of the Seven Vowels"* Joscelyn Godwin has included an account from the Roman architectural writer Vitruvius who observed that some Roman theatres had bronze vases tuned to different notes placed around the stage. When a singer sang the same note as the resonant frequency of the cavity of the vase it would amplify the voice. These vessels were very possibly the first speakers in the world! You can experience the power of amplification by sympathetic resonance first-hand. Next time you are in the shower start singing in a low tone and slide slowly up to a higher tone. When you reach the resonant frequency of the shower cubicle you will hear the shower begin to sing with you! It's easier to do this in a small space if you are on your own, or get a group of people together and explore churches, caves and other spaces. It is the most wonderful feeling to interact with a space in this way.

The engineers that built the Millennium Bridge in London were very proud of their construction until shortly after the opening ceremony. As people began walking across the bridge it started swaying at an alarming rate! The "wobbly bridge" was immediately closed and engineers began an investigation into what had happened. According to a report from the BBC it was finally blamed on *"synchronous lateral excitation due to the synchronized footfall of hundreds of people walking in unison"*. The energy frequency of the footsteps of the walkers resonated with the fabric of the bridge, causing it to sway. The solution was to fit 91 inertial dampeners very similar to the shock absorbers on a car to the bridge. These absorbed the energy generated by people's footsteps and the bridge was reopened in January 2002.

We use the metaphor "on the same wavelength" when people feel a connection with each other on some level. This is sympathetic resonance, which is more of an instant like or attraction to any thing or person, rather than something that happens over time. In the field of physics the positive energy of sympathetic resonance is known as *"constructive interference"* and the negative energy is known as *"destructive interference"*. In *"The Biology of Belief"*, Dr Bruce Lipton uses the analogy of two pebbles being dropped into water to describe constructive and destructive interference. Where the ripples made by the pebbles overlap there will be a convergence. If the pebbles are dropped from different heights or at different times (or both) the waves will be out of synch when they overlap so one wave will be going up when the other is going down. This results in the energy within the waves cancelling each other out. This *"destructive interference"* has an energy draining effect. When the pebbles are coordinated and dropped from the same height at the same time, the energy of the waves will be doubled at the place where they overlap. This *"constructive interference"* is energy enhancing.

When exploring some of the exercises later in this book you may find sympathetic resonance occurring as your system interacts with the sound. Your chakras may resonate with a particular sound in a particular way which will give you an indication of how to conduct your sounding sessions. With practice you will become more aware of the resonances in your system as you go about your daily tasks. This is when the true transformation can take place.

"Entrainment is defined as the tendency for two oscillating bodies to lock into phase so that they vibrate in harmony. It is also defined as a synchronization of two or more rhythmic cycles."
Collins English Dictionary

Entrainment

The history of entrainment goes back to a Dutch scientist named Christian Huygens. In 1661, whilst working on the design of the pendulum clock, Huygens found that when many clocks were placed together in the same room over time they would synchronize, even though they started swinging at different rates.

The entrainment process appears in every area of our lives. Usually it is the most dominant frequency that others entrain to and, as with Huygens' clocks the strongest clock brought the others in to line with itself. With regard to the "wobbly bridge" mentioned in the previous section, the entrainment principle also came into play. After examining video footage of people walking across the bridge engineers noticed that after a few moments many of the people on the bridge began to walk in step with each other. This was an unconscious demonstration of the entrainment principle that could have had devastating consequences.

Just as we are entraining others, we are being entrained by outside influences all the time. Women living in close proximity will often find that their menstrual cycles will synchronize; couples sharing the same bed tend to breathe at the same rate whilst sleeping; people sharing a conversation may mirror body language and a fast paced drum beat will cause your heart-rate and blood pressure to increase.

The entrainment principle is not just confined to planet Earth.

The ancient practice of Astrology is based on the subtle entraining effects that the planets and heavenly bodies exert on us. Pythagoras of Samos was born in the 6th century BC. And although he was not the first (many ancient civilizations such as the Egyptians and Mayans had different systems) he was arguably the most well-known person to base a system of health and wellbeing on the entraining influence of the subtle energy of the planets and other heavenly bodies. Plato, Newton and Kepler also deliberated, discussed and developed their own systems and theories of how the music of the spheres influenced us at a fundamental level. We know that the moon has an entraining effect on the tides and plants and it also influences us. The word "lunatic" was used to describe a person who was affected on the mental and emotional levels by the moon.

When we communicate with others the entrainment principle is at work. The latest neurological research has shown that the limbic system in the brain is an "open loop" system, in contrast to our circulation, which is a "closed loop" system. The open loop of the limbic system means that when two or more people get together our limbic systems synchronize, allowing for a greater level of communication to take place. In *"The New Leaders"*, Daniel Goleman, et.al, states *"the continual interplay of limbic open loops among members of a group creates a kind of emotional soup, with everyone adding his or her own flavour to the mix. But it is the leader who adds the strongest seasoning."* I believe this is why thought-shower sessions can be so fruitful.

In every day life the entrainment principle is everywhere. From advertisements on the television persuading us to change our shampoo to peers encouraging us to support the same football team, entrainment is a natural part of life and we cannot avoid it. Entrainment can be positively or negatively charged and each of us responds differently to the same stimulus. For example, you may like watching the daily news bulletins, eating garlic bread and listening to gangster rap, but your friend may have negatively charged energetic reactions to some or all of these. Manipulation, brainwashing or any other technique which sways you from your original path is another example of entrainment. You can often identify the negative aspects of this principle by an uncomfortable feeling in the solar plexus.

When sounding the mind of God the laws of sympathetic resonance and entrainment are key. Therapeutic sound has the potential to resonate with your energy system on all levels, transforming negativity into positivity and promoting a state of calm or stimulation. Through constructive interference sound can expand your energy system, which in turn raises consciousness. Sound can also help transport the listener from one place to another so could be seen as facilitating a process that is out of space and time.

Exercise: Sympathetic resonance and entrainment

Aim: The aim of this exercise is to become familiar with the principles of sympathetic resonance and entrainment and identify where they are occurring in your life.

Make a list headed "sympathetic resonance". Under this heading list three or four examples when you have instantly been attracted to something or someone in your life. Add to this list when sympathetic resonance occurs over the next couple of weeks.

Make another list headed "entrainment". Under this heading list three or more examples when you feel you have been negatively entrained by something or someone and list three instances when you have entrained others negatively. Try to expand these instances beyond people or events and include addictions and habits. An example of negative entrainment which becomes a habit or addiction could be when your mother repeatedly told you to eat all of your dinner and "not to be so wasteful". If you have issues with food or wasting things then this could be where it came from. If your friend convinced you to start smoking because it was the "cool" thing to do this is another example of being entrained by others. Or perhaps you were the one who convinced your friend to start smoking? If this is the case, this is an example where you have used the power of entrainment to influence others. Remember it is only negative if you see it that way. Do the same for positive entrainment. After a couple of weeks look back and see if there are any patterns showing up.

"Contraction records memory. By making each egoic cell smaller, the world becomes larger and unfriendly. Each unit, in diminishing itself, actually programmes itself for self-annihilation."
Fred Alan Wolf PhD

Radiators, Drains and the Universal Breath

In the previous chapter we learned that constructive interference is expanding and destructive interference is draining therefore you could say that constructive energy is positive and destructive energy is negative. The words "positive" and "negative" can imply that something is "good" or "bad". But even the most destructive energy can be positive as it often comes with a wonderful opportunity for growth and learning. I prefer to avoid looking at energy in terms of "good" and "bad" therefore I will be referring to the different polarities of energy as being "positively charged" and "negatively charged".

Everything is based on the principles of expansion and contraction, constriction and release, density and fineness. Cosmologists have observed the planets and stars moving away from the source of the big bang at an ever increasing velocity. If you look at the expansion of the big bang as being a "great exhale", perhaps one day the heavenly bodies will reach their limit. Maybe there will be a "big inhale", where everything in the universe contracts back to one single point as if each star and planet were on an invisible bungee cord. Or perhaps the expansion will continue and one day our world will be an isolated desolate sphere hanging alone in the inky blackness. Scientists have postulated both theories and the latter seems to be the favorite, but I'm straying from the point. The point is that most living systems breathe in some way. We breathe in and out, hold on and let go. The tides ebb and flow and flowers open and close.

Constriction & Release Diagram

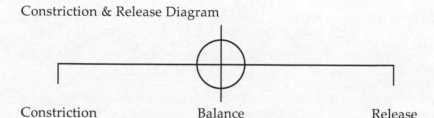

Constriction   Balance   Release

Imagine a line with constriction on the far left and expansion on the far right. With regard to your health and wellbeing all symptoms are to be found somewhere along this line. An example of a constricting symptom could be arthritis or consti- pation, anything that has a nature of holding on, closing down or making small. Symptoms which are a manifestation of release can be anything that implies lack of boundary, flowing, watery, running away and multiplying rapidly such as M.E, diarrhea and some immune system disorders. I was tempted to include a table of symptoms and their energetic tendencies in this book but I am resistant to making too many generalizations when dis-ease can manifest as a result of so many factors. Hopefully you will be able to figure out where your symptom is on the constriction and release line, but don't worry too much if you are not sure or if your symptom seems to embrace both elements, such as IBS which can result in a person experiencing both diarrhea and constipation. As you work through this book hopefully things will become clearer. The beauty of sound work is that sometimes we don't need to know what is going on. With clear and focused intention the sound will be directed to where it needs to go. The most important thing at this stage is for you to find out how positively and negatively charged energy affects you.

Exercise: Identifying expansion and contraction

Aim: The aim of this exercise is for you to feel the effects of positively and negatively charged energy. Read this exercise first and then close your eyes and fully immerse yourself in the process.

Recall an event in your life when you were really happy, positive and on top of your game. It could be the time you first fell in love or won an award. Fill your mind, body and spirit with this feeling. Now multiply it by ten, breathing in the feeling on all levels of being. When you have filled your entire being with this feeling, cast your mind immediately to something that you recently saw on television or read in the newspapers that shocked you. It could have been a natural disaster or a murder or war, anything of this nature. Once again feel it in on all levels of being. After a few moments, bring your thoughts back to the wonderful event in your life and fill your being with this feeling once more before bringing your awareness back to the here and now.

How did that feel?

Make two columns headed "positively charged" and "negatively charged". In the positive column note down all the words that came to you to describe how you felt during the first visualization. Under the negative column list the words that describe your experience during the second visualization.

People often use words like *"light"* (in both color and weight), *"bright"*, *"happy"*, *"energizing"*, *"nourishing"* and *"joyful"* to describe the positive visualization and *"heavy"*, *"dark"*, *"depressing"*, *"hateful"*, *"fearful"*, *"disempowering"* and *"draining"* to describe the negative visualization. Reflect on how you felt on each level of your being. Did you feel physically heavy or light in weight? Was your mind clear or confused? How did you feel emotionally? Stretch your awareness as much as you can. Did you feel the vitality and quality of your spiritual body? Some use the word "expanded" and "contracted" to describe how their spiritual level responded to this exercise. Remember the destructive and constructive interference we discussed earlier? This is exactly the principle that is at work when your energy responds to these visualizations.

For the benefit of this exercise I used two extremes but your system is responding all the time in varying degrees somewhere along the expansion/contraction line. Once you have experienced the way your system responds to these extremes you are then able to sensitize yourself to feeling the more subtle changes in your field.

Some of your daily activities may have a draining effect on the different levels of your being and others will radiate positive energy and will therefore feed you. The following exercise is similar to the previous one, but enables you to discover how your daily life affects the different levels of your being. You can then see the areas that require balance and make changes accordingly.

Exercise: Radiators and drains

Aim: The aim of this exercise is to identify which activities in your daily life radiate and which drain.

Divide a page in your journal into two columns headed "radiators" and "drains". Take time to think about your daily activities as thoroughly as you can. Include people, foods, habits, events, venues (such as pubs, shops, sports centers and towns) and television programs and so on. Feel each activity resonate in the system. If it is positively charged and expands your energy list it under "radiators" and if it is negatively charged and contracting, list it under "drains". If you have any that are neutral you can make another column or leave them out.

After completing these two exercises hopefully you will have a good idea of how positive and negatively charged energy affects you as well as how your daily activities resonate in your system.

If you have more activities in your "drains" column then it is likely that you are feeling low in energy. You may also have developed symptoms due to the amount of denser energy in your system inhibiting the free-flowing of prana, especially if you have been adopting a draining lifestyle for a long period of time. If this is the case, aim to bring balance back into your life by increasing the items in your "radiators" column and reducing the activities that drain you. If you have more items in your "drains" column but are not feeling it yet then you could be running on reserve so the sooner you begin radiating, the better!

People ask me if you can have too much positively charged energy. This is an interesting question. As a holistic practitioner I aim to help my clients to achieve balance and therefore too much of anything could be seen as imbalance, although I have never yet met anyone who was suffering from having too much positive energy. I have seen individuals who find it difficult to remain grounded in the here and now and there can be many different reasons for this such as overactive energy in the head, imbalances in the chakras and/or on the different levels of being. I tend to go by the old saying "if it ain't broke, don't fix it". If an individual is not displaying symptoms on any level of being that would indicate an imbalance then all is well. Through the principle of entrainment we know that the energy system can become challenged by outside influences so it doesn't hurt to maintain even the most balanced of systems with regular sound therapy exercises.

"This etheric field is generated by the totality of internal processes – from the energetic exchange of subatomic particles to the digestion of food in our cells, from the firing of neurons to our current emotional state and on to the larger rhythms of our outer activities."
Anodea Judith

The Auric Field

The traditional view of the aura was that it was a division between us and the outside world, like an invisible force-field, but we now know this is not the case. The auric field is an extension of you and is connected to all that is. Part 1 of this book encourages you to divide yourself into levels to help identify whereabouts in your energy system an imbalance is manifesting. This helps our logical human minds to devise a sonic prescription to suit our needs and allows us to achieve a greater sense of awareness, but energy by its very nature is not confined to the different levels of our being. Each aspect of us is continually

The Auric Field

communicating with the other as well as the universe beyond our physical form.

We have previously explored the different levels of being and how they have different densities. We know that the floor is 'energetically' denser than the air as we are unable to breathe the floor or walk on the air but we also know that everything, no matter how dense or fine, is made of resonating particles and waves of energy. This energy is not confined to the object, nor is our energy solely confined to our bodies and therefore aspects of us are communicating with the floor and the air all of the time and vice-versa. This may explain how some people are able to feel the energy radiating from a crystal or sense that there has been an argument when they walk into a room. A saying that is often used is "you can cut the atmosphere with a knife". This accurately describes the dense energy that is present following a negatively charged experience such as an argument or sad news.

The mystery of matter is something that has perplexed scientists for many years. If we are all made from particles and waves of energy how do we stick together? This is still a matter of debate among physicists who are hoping they will find the answers inside the Large Hadron Collider (LHC) based at CERN in Geneva, Switzerland. By colliding quantum particles they are hoping to discover the elusive Higgs Boson, a particle which has been dubbed "the God particle" which physicists believe may have a part to play in the creation of mass.

By monitoring your energy system and keeping it balanced the lines of communication between you and the mind of God are enhanced. This increased level of communication enables you to transform your life in the most profound ways. It is easy to say, but how is this *actually* possible? In Lynne Taggarts book, "The Field" Lynne includes this wonderful quote from two researchers. *"Every time you use your toaster, the fields around it perturb charged particles in the farthest galaxies ever so slightly"*. I believe this describes the interconnectedness of energy perfectly.

I have never used my toaster in quite the same way since!

This principle of connectedness is known in the world of quantum physics as "entanglement". Through the entanglement principle two or more seemingly unconnected points can be connected through space and time. The way one entangled particle behaves will directly affect its twin which could account for the psychic connection that some people who are close to each other have as well as a host of other phenomena, including distant healing. When it comes to the process of transformation and wholing it is unavoidable that when you make any change to your inner world your outer world changes too.

Because of the wonderful nature of energy we know that there is no separation between you and this book, the floor, your neighbor, the Earth and the Universe. We are all one in an energy soup of consciousness. This energy soup is known by many names including the "quantum vacuum" (QV), the "zero point field", the "Higgs field", the "Source", the "Akasha", the "universal consciousness" and the "mind of God".

Exercise: Feeling the Aura
Aim: The aim of this exercise is to familiarize yourself with your auric field.

Rub your hands together palm to palm for ten seconds or so. This action increases the sensitivity in the hands and palm chakras. Take your hands apart to about shoulder width in front of you with your palms facing each other. Bring your hands slowly together as if praying but don't let them touch. Then take your hands apart and back together in a slow and gentle bouncing movement. Imagine you are holding an invisible ball of energy which is becoming more tangible the more you work with it. Your hands may begin to feel hot, tingly and prickly, or you may notice a number of other sensations. Some people feel a slight resistance similar to when the same poles of a magnet are brought together. This is your auric field.

You are able to feel the energy between your hands because the energy closest to the physical body is dense enough to enable you to feel it. You may already be able to see the colors of the auric field but, if you can't, as you work with the exercises in this book you may find that your visual spectrum increases in sensitivity, allowing the colors of the aura to become visible.

"To believe natural processes assembles a living cell is like believing a tornado could pass through a junk yard containing the bits and pieces of an airplane and leave a Boeing 747 in its wake, fully assembled and ready to fly!"
Fred Hoyle

Energetic Blueprints, Consciousness and Intention

What makes an oak tree an oak or a birch tree a birch? They are both made of the same "stuff" (wood, sap etc) so why are they different? There is a growing amount of scientific evidence to support the idea that everything conforms to different patterns or blueprints. The developmental biologist Rupert Sheldrake calls these blueprints *"morphogenetic fields"*, and states that *"these fields evolve and form part of a collective and instinctive memory"*. Harold Saxton Burr, a professor at Yale found that a salamander egg has an electromagnetic field around it in the form of an adult salamander even before it is fertilized. Salamanders have long been the subject of research due to their ability to re-grow their limbs and tail. The existence of energetic blueprints could help explain why a salamander knows exactly how much limb or tail to re-grow. It is as if the salamander grows back into the original energetic blueprint of itself. Human limb regeneration is also feasible and it has already been proven that amputated fingers can grow back if the wound is cleaned and dressed simply, rather than sutured closed. According to an article in Scientific American published in March 2008, *"human beings have inherent regenerative capabilities that, sadly, have been suppressed by some of our traditional medical practices."* It makes perfect sense that if you stitch the wounded finger closed you are preventing the energy in the finger from enabling the regeneration process to take place.

We know that a birch tree has a blueprint that organizes the wood and leaves into the shape and characteristics that tell us it is a birch. Let's call this the "overall energetic blueprint". As well as the overall energetic blueprint, there will also be other factors which will have a bearing on the health of the tree such as the location, weather and soil condition. It is the same in the world of humans. One person's heart has the same biological make up as the heart of another but there are also individual characteristics that make the heart different such as the age, level of fitness and the general health of the heart. In the chapter on "radiators and drains", we learned that positively charged energy has a nourishing and expanding effect on the system and that negatively charged energy is draining and can pull us "out of tune" over time. Through negative entrainment your blueprint could be altered over time by negatively charged energy in the form of thoughts, words, actions, diet, lifestyle and a host of other influences.

As a fetus develops in the womb there is something that gives each cell the instruction to grow into a heart, blood, bone or eye, but *what*? What brought us into being? What told us to crawl from the primordial slime and to eventually evolve from primates into humans?

In his book *"Intelligent Life"*, the British astrophysicist Fred Hoyle stated that the odds that life was created "by accident" without any conscious intervention are really low. The great debate is what or who is behind this wonderful creation? Some of us believe that a powerful force in the form of a God or Goddess created the universe. Others are firmly against there being a force behind creation and with the remainder the jury is out. I believe that this is the missing piece of the jigsaw puzzle that has compelled us to connect with the divine force since we first appeared on Mother Earth. It is the innate feeling that there is something "more" that has driven us to creation and destruction, bliss and fear, feast and famine. We feel it right down in the core of our being.

The creation/evolution debate continues and in my opinion both are right to a certain extent. I believe that we're created by a manipulation of *consciously directed energy*.

We have already discovered that the objects around us are made from particles and waves which exist in a state of potential. In the past it was thought that we were small parts in the great machine of life and that we had no influence over what happened to us, but as the worlds of science and spirituality are meeting this view is changing. For thousands of years Eastern spiritual teachings have said that we have a direct impact on our reality. But to what extent do we influence the world around us?

Our conscious mind helps bring the waves of energy that previously existed in a state of potential into actuality. This is known by quantum physicists as "collapsing the wave-function". The collapse of the wave into the particle causes it to split momentarily from the wave. If you were to video rain falling into a puddle you would be seeing the drops (particles) falling into and becoming one with the puddle (the wave). The puddle becomes a mass of drops but the drops cease to have their own identity. If you were to rewind the video you would see the drop split back out of the puddle and travel back up towards the sky. This is what happens when the wave collapses. When a particle is observed it suddenly splits from the wave and becomes an object, in this case, an individual drop. Each individual drop of energy is then shaped by consciousness into a given object, feeling, event etc. As we are all part of the quantum soup, this collapse of the wave-function is also where "we" become "I". In *"Matter into Feeling"*, Dr Fred Alan Wolf states that *"consciousness seems to be a process where an environment and an observer of that environment become defined simultaneously"*. He also goes on to say that it *"requires some kind of awareness and causes a split between the subject and object, between the "out there" and the "in here"*. If you sit quietly and observe your thoughts you will notice that you cannot control them one hundred percent of the time. This is another example of the subject/object split, the time when you are the thinker and when your thoughts are thinking you.

In *"The Self-aware Universe"*, Amit Goswami states that *"without the immanent world of manifestation, there would be no soul, no self that experiences itself as separate from the objects it perceives."* So not only are you inextricably linked to everything that is but you are also influencing everything around you as your consciousness collapses the wave-function, enabling you to experience your reality in the way that you do. If you are constantly influencing your reality to that extent, it makes perfect sense that as your awareness changes, so does your reality.

Consciousness exists outside of the brain as well as inside. Imagine that consciousness is like radio waves in the atmosphere. You cannot see the waves but they are all around you and contain a wealth of information which you filter through the different levels of your being. The morphogenetic fields are physical blueprints, but there are also blueprints containing instinctual and learned behavior. In *"The Field"* Lynne Mc Taggart states *"the more we learn, the easier it is for others to follow in our footsteps"*. This makes absolute sense. By aligning to the mind of God we can benefit from information that has been stored in these blueprints over lifetimes. As each of us learns our lessons and feeds our experience into the mind of God we add to the overall fundamental frequency of the field. Therefore the more we expand our energy, the more we will affect others around us through the principle of sympathetic resonance and entrainment.

Perhaps the ability to align to these all-knowing blueprints has influenced some of the great scientific discoveries, inventions and quantum leaps in our technology. The great scientists, doctors and inventors could have gained insight by unconsciously aligning to the mind of God. It is interesting that many of the greatest discoveries were made when the person was in a relaxed state, or not even thinking about their work. Archimedes was in the bath when he had his Eureka moment (as was I when I first realized the wholing power of the voice), Pythagoras discovered the harmonic series as he was walking by a blacksmith's shop and Newton discovered his second law (gravity) when he was visiting his mother's apple farm. This would make perfect sense. Being in a more relaxed state enables the alignment process to take place.

In the spiritual world, this alignment process was (and still is) facilitated by prayers and other meditative practices. Thousands of years ago Hindu mystics taught their students about the existence of the Akashic records. "*Akasha*" is Sanskrit for "ether", "sky" or "space". The Akashic records contain a recording of everything that has ever happened or will happen. As these records exist in the fourth dimension they are outside space and time. Some say that they even contain the knowledge of beings that inhabit other planets and dimensions. Interestingly, the Akashic records have also been called the "mind of God" but it doesn't matter what name we give to this field of consciousness, the most important thing is to know that it is a fountain of knowledge that is available to all and by practicing simple exercises we are able to drink deeply.

The observer effect

In the field of quantum physics it is known that the outcome of some scientific experiments can change depending on the expectations of the scientist conducting the experiment. This is known as the "observer effect" and shows that at a quantum level we can affect our reality. We also know that a person can directly influence their body chemistry, and therefore their health, by thought alone. At the level of thought shifts in consciousness can directly affect our health and our lives. This revolutionary discovery has fundamentally altered the way we look at the world.

To summarize, everything exists in a state of potential until our consciousness shapes our reality. When sound and this belief come together this creates a potent mixture which helps align us to a world of wonder where anything and everything is possible and quantum wholing can take place. In his book *"Healing Sounds"*, Jonathan Goldman includes the following formula to illustrate the importance of intention when working with sound.

Frequency + Intention = Healing

He goes on to say *"I am convinced that this formula is correct and that without the aspect of intention, working with pure frequency alone is not the answer"*.

Masaru Emoto's work illustrated that water can be manipulated by the vibrational changes that our thoughts and feelings transmit. In his book *"The Hidden Messages in Water"* Emoto refers to the water in our bodies as the *"master listener"*. He illustrates that water can hold an intention by subjecting it to positively or negatively charged energy in the form of a word written on the side of a phial that contains a sample of water. In some experiments, music and sound was also played to the water. The water was then frozen and the ice crystals were photographed with very interesting results. The intention behind the word, music or emotion was transferred to the water in the phial. The positively charged energy created beautiful symmetrical crystals and the negatively charged energy created distorted and sometimes dark crystals. Emoto's work clearly demonstrated that intention in its purest form (thought) when carried by words or sounds can directly influence matter, in this case water.

The average human body is approximately 70 per cent water. Water is a very good carrier of sound, which is illustrated by the fact that whale song can be heard for miles underwater and yet doesn't carry very far in the air. When considering the results of Emoto's experiments it doesn't take a rocket scientist to work out what happens to us on an energetic level when we are subjected to negatively charged energy carried by words or actions.

"What things soever ye desire, when we pray, believe that ye receive them, and ye shall have them" Mark 11:24

According to Dr Wayne Dyer in *"The Power of Intention"* repeating the word *"intent"* or *"intention"* will help you to shape your reality and reinforce your alignment to the mind of God. In my experience, the more you feel the God-force resonating within you the more you realize that the only separation between you and what you want *is you*. *You* are the only thing keeping *you* from realizing *your* dreams. If this statement activates resistance within you, wonderful! Explore the resistance as it may enable you to open to another world of potential. A little later on I will introduce some techniques which I hope will make the exploration process more enlightening.

When I hear people say *"you can't have everything"* a little voice inside me says *"why not?"* If you believe that you can't have everything then you won't; it is that simple. I am now going to contradict myself, but I also believe that when you become enlightened you don't want *everything*. Trying to define ourselves with personal possessions is in itself a form of separation as the ego becomes involved, but more about this later.

The film *"The Secret"* was based around the principle of manifestation. One of the principles of manifesting your heart's desire is by aligning to the belief that you already have what you want. By doing this you are opening up to receiving whatever you want into your life. This is very good in principle but what if this doesn't work for you? People sometimes say to me "I've tried all of those manifestation techniques and my life is still the same!"

I believe that we all have the ability to manifest what we want in life, and we do, all of the time. We think we don't want it, but if we've got it, it is because we have aligned to it (whatever *it* is). On some level we have manifested it as part of our life experience. Every experience is an opportunity to learn and grow and you are sending yourself messages all of the time in the form of life experiences, physical symptoms and challenges. You shape your reality according to your belief system. So when you have spent hours cosmic ordering yourself a pair of designer shoes, a new partner and a sports car and you are still waiting for them to arrive it is because there is a limiting belief that is holding you back. All you need to do is a bit of re-programming.

Exercise – Attracting what you want

Aim: The aim of this exercise is to identify limiting beliefs.

Make a list of everything that you want as if you already have it. When you have finished, state each one out loud three times and listen for resonances on any level of your being. Are there some statements that you cannot align to? If so, set up the enquiry to get to the root of the statement. For example;

"I am incredibly rich" - *"no you're not"* pipes up an inner voice. This is the resistance so begin communicating with it. Don't think too much about it, just take the first answer that comes to you.

Why?   *"because I am always scraping around for money"*
Why?   *"because I can't get a good job"*
Why?   *"because I'll never be able to get the job I want"*
Why?   *"because I'm not good enough"*

Bingo! Here we have the core message underneath the belief. This person will never be incredibly rich unless they are able to transcend this pattern. When they do, they may become incredibly rich, or they may not actually want to be incredibly rich as their priorities may have changed. Either way they have manifested their heart's desire without resistance.

Work through every one of the statements that produce a negatively charged resonance within your being. If you have a lot of statements choose the ones that produce the strongest reaction. You may find that by clearing the resistance around the most intensely charged statements some of the other statements are also less charged. This is an indication that these statements were connected on some level. Don't worry if you cannot see the connection; the most important thing is that you have transcended the resistance. Once you begin working in this way life has the potential to change very fast.

"Once is an accident, twice is unlucky and three times is a pattern"
Source unknown

Personal Filters and Energetic Roundabouts

To what extent do we shape our universe? Can we *really* manifest anything we want?

We have already discovered that we experience our world depending on our personal programs. Imagine you are flying over a motorway where there is a huge traffic jam. You are gifted with X-ray vision which enables you to see through the top of the cars and you choose four cars to peer into. In car one you see a women painting her nails and enjoying a little pampering time. In car two there is an angry young executive who is on the verge of chewing through the steering wheel with the stress of being stuck in the jam when he should be in an important meeting. Car three contains a couple who is having a kiss and cuddle and in car four is a parent who is enjoying spending some extra time with her children.

In these four cars pleasure, anger, stress, joy and love is being experienced as a result of the same event. We all react differently to our world. Each event you experience only becomes positively or negatively charged depending on the reaction you have to the situation. If you have no reaction, the event is neutral to you. If you have a positive reaction, this creates a feeling of expansion in the system as it is resonating with the positive energy within you. If you have a negative reaction, this is because the energy of the event is resonating with negative energy within you. If you are feeling angry, sad or jealous it is only because you have something within you for these emotions to resonate with. Once you have transmuted the negatively charged energy within, situations that may have previously triggered negatively charged reactions become neutral or even positive.

Have you ever felt you were being presented with the same scenario or challenge in your life? These recurring life-limiting events are known as "holding patterns". You think you have learned a lesson and wham, there it is again! It may have conned you into thinking it was different. It may have been presented in a slightly different package, but when you peel off the gift-wrapping you find it is the same pair of moldy old socks! I use this analogy because our patterns really are gifts; they are opportunities for personal wholing and transformation.

A pattern is learned behavior that develops as a result of an event that we experience, but it can also be learned by osmosis through a third party. For example, I put my hand in the fire, I burn my hand, it hurts and blisters. I have learned that fire hurts and injures me. I can then choose whether or not to put my hand in the fire again. Or, I approach the fire and I am told sternly by an adult not to go near the fire or it will burn me. At this point I choose not to go near fire again. If the behavior of the adult is extreme I may develop a fear of fire without even having a direct experience of being burned myself. One could argue that this would only happen if there were fear inside me on some level that resonated with the fear of the adult telling me to keep away from the fire. Kolb's Learning Cycle (1976) can be used to illustrate how an individual makes sense of their world, and how patterns can be formed.

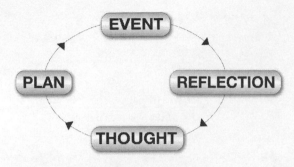

Kolb's Learning Cycle

Event	A person experiences an event
Reflection	They reflect on the event
Thought	The person thinks about the experience and develops a concept based on the experience
Plan	The behavior, body chemistry and ultimately the health of the person is altered depending on the experience.

For example

Event	You have a fight with a friend because they tell you that you are fat
Reflection	You run the scenario over in your head, reflecting back on their words and the words of others that have told you the same in the past
Thought	You begin to believe you are fat
Plan	Your body chemistry may have been altered as a result of your self-belief, which may alter your behavior around food, and your belief about your body.

And so the pattern runs…

Underneath a pattern you can usually find the culprit, a "core message". The first step is to recognize the pattern and then identify the core message underneath. The second step is to transmute the energy around the pattern with your alignment and sounding sessions. As a result the energy around the pattern becomes less dense, allowing yourself and your outer world to change.

In her book *"Toning"*, Laurelle Elizabeth Keyes has included the following quote from Dr William Tiller *"all illness has its origin in a disharmony between the mind and spirit levels of the entity and that of the universal pattern for the entity. Thus healing at the physical or even the etheric level is only temporary if the basic pattern at the mind and spirit level remains unchanged"*.

Every time something occurs in your life which reinforces your core message it is like running another loop of the pattern. I call these energetic roundabouts. If you were to drive a car round and round in circles in the dirt, after a while you will wear some pretty deep grooves. You may even get to the point where you are able to take your hands off the wheel and let the car steer itself!

If we examine energy at the different levels of being we know that the finer something is the easier it is to transmute (the fewer times you have driven the car round in the dirt the easier it is to change direction). After a while the grooves become deeper and it is going to be a bit bumpy to change direction, but no big deal. Once you have worn yourself some deep grooves the chances are the denser levels of the physical body are being affected and therefore more work is needed to change direction so the sooner you can identify the groove you are in, the better. Even if you have worn a pretty deep groove, don't worry. The alignment and sounding sessions will help you to smooth out your path ahead.

Earlier in this book we looked at listening to the messages that the different levels of our being have for us and you may have noted some of these down in your journal. If the same message has come up time and again, this points to a pattern. For example, Chloe had experienced several difficult relationships starting with her father and then with several men in her early adulthood. Every time a relationship "went bad" she reflected on it and began to think *"it must be me"*. If she was snubbed in some way when she interacted with men this added to her core message *"no one finds me attractive, I can't get the good ones, it must be me!"* As a result she began to send out the thought-wave *"I can't get the good ones"*. This altered her behavior around men, and lo and behold she attracted men that were not good for her which perpetuated the cycle.

Other very common core messages can be related to self-worth such as *"I don't deserve to be healthy/happy/wealthy"* for instance. If you are ignoring any of the messages you are getting during your tuning-in sessions have a look to see if there is a pattern holding you. I am not suggesting that you need to make radical changes to your life if it does not feel right for you, but be open to change when the time is right. Being aware that there is a pattern that is holding you means that you are over half-way to personal transformation.

Exercise: Identifying your energetic roundabouts

Aim: The aim of this exercise is to help increase self-awareness by identifying the holding patterns in your life and how they affect the different levels of being. Once you are aware of the underlying patterns you can begin working on them with sound. Patterns often "leak out" in our language; not only the spoken word but also our body language and how we relate to others. Have a look at the following list, identify any resonances and answer the following questions.

Verbal language	*"I can't do this", "See, I told you I was useless", "I'm so ugly/fat/skinny"*
Body language	Holding and positioning of the body, holding the breath, crossing arms over the solar plexus, clasping the throat, clenching the fists or jaw etc.
Behavior	Repetition of behavior, constricted behavior, limiting your energy in certain areas.

Ego   The ego state can teach you a lot about
                        yourself and highlight your core messages.
                        How separate do you feel from yourself
                        and/or others? Do you think you are egotis-
                        tical? If so, which situations trigger this
                        response?

Do you have struggles with money, relationships, success, insecurity or anger? Write down the challenges you have that come immediately to mind, and then add to the list over the coming week. At the end of the week reflect on what you have written down and see if you can identify any patterns.

You can be in a relationship that does not feed you and you know you need to get out, but packing your bags there and then may not be the best way forward for you. You may need to make plans regarding where to live or sort out financial arrangements before making your move. When everything is in alignment you will make the choice easily and smoothly and things will fall into place. The perfect house may become available or a job opportunity may present itself. Being open to change is often enough to send signals out into the universe and transmute the energy in your life. You will know when you are avoiding the messages that you are telling yourself. It is up to you to choose whether or not to embrace change.

Unconscious patterns can also be dense as these are buried deep in the psyche. By raising your awareness and expanding your energy there is no reason why even the most stubborn unconscious patterns can be transmuted. As awareness increases sometimes dense, unconscious patterns pop into consciousness, and sometimes they are transmuted without our even knowing what happened. In her book, *"Molecules of Emotion"*, Candace Pert explains that *"the unconscious mind of the body seems all-knowing and all-powerful and in some therapies can be harnessed for healing or change without the conscious mind ever figuring out what happened.*" In my experience, this is often the case and in essence it does not really matter. Often people like to know where something comes from or why an imbalance is there.

When I am giving a treatment I first scan the energy system of my client with sound which highlights the areas that I need to concentrate on. I then share my findings with the client and explain how I am going to proceed with their treatment. If there is a large imbalance over the left knee, for example, this may point to an injury. If the client cannot remember the injury taking place sometimes I get the sense that this is causing them to worry about where the imbalance came from as they have no story behind it. This defeats the object of the treatment which is to help the client transmute negatively charged energy! If you find yourself needing to attach to the meaning of something, let it go.

We love a good story. Stories help us maintain the illusion of the ego-self by reinforcing our meaning. As we go through life we add to our story as we grow and develop. If you have seen the film *"Jaws"* you may remember Richard Dreyfuss and Robert Shaw sitting in the boat comparing the scars that they received from encounters with various creatures of the deep. Each scar has a story to tell that reinforces their personal identity. It reminds them that they are alive, "stronger than", "better than", "cleverer than", etc. For them this is an ego inflating experience. On the surface they are feeling wonderful, but deep down they are separating themselves from the universal source, which ultimately causes pain and suffering.

The particle boogie

The root of many of our patterns can come from the struggle of the ego to stay separate. In Fred Alan Wolf's book *"Matter into Feeling"* Wolf includes quotes from some of the great philosophers and teachers. Adida Sam Raj considers the Freudian ego to be a *"devastating construct that keeps human beings from realising their God-selves"*. Paramahansa Yogananda describes the ego as *"the root cause of dualism – the seeming separation between man and his creator".*

I believe that it is the illusion of separation that causes resistance, pain and suffering. We know that matter is made from "trapped light". In *"Matter into Feeling"* Wolf explains that even the quantum particles that we are made of have egos and that our feelings can be easily explained in terms of the *"matter-light transformation of electrons"*. He states that *"hate is connected with the fact that no two electrons will ever exist in the same quantum state....electrons composed of trapped light desire freedom. Electrons "feel" some form of suffering because of this confinement"*. He goes on to explain that our suffering is a result of the desire that the electrons have to be free and become particles of light (photons).

The photons within us are particles of light that naturally want to move together in harmonic resonance and create more light. Wolf has dubbed the photon the *"love particle"* as it displays properties of unconditional love. According to Wolf the photon *"represents people tending to be in a unified state of consciousness, for example, lovers being of like minds, or becoming one with God"*. From this explanation we are able to understand that aligning to the mind of God allows you to become en-lightened, to keep your light "topped up" and to move with the unconditional love vibration of the photon. Perhaps this explains the "particle boogie" that we are continually doing, the dance between the need to be an individual with an identity and the need to be part of something greater than ourselves.

"If you found yourself in paradise, it wouldn't be long before your mind would say "yes, but....." Ultimately this is not about solving your problems. It's about realizing that there are no problems."
Eckhart Tolle

What We Believe and Why

We have already discovered that each of us views our world in different ways and develops different concepts based on our experience. We also know that these concepts can be life limiting and ultimately affect our health and wellbeing. In this section we will examine different methods of enquiry which aim to identify and help resolve imbalances that originated at the level of thought and, depending on how they have been reinforced, may now also be held on other levels of being.

The following enquiry is really simple and is based on the Socratic method of dialogue named after the Greek philosopher Socrates. Similar techniques are also used by cognitive behavior therapists as well as Adlerian psychologists.

Exercise: The enquiry

Aim: The following exercise is very useful when something in your outer world triggers something within.

Write down the statement that you are thinking or feelings you are having. Start the sentence off with *"I am feeling ...."*

Identify why you are feeling that way and then continue with *"And this means that..............."*

If you make a statement and you need more clarity, ask "why?" This may take your enquiry to another level. You may well find that other core messages or beliefs raise their heads during this process and you can always go back and address them separately, but keep going with this until you cannot go any further.

Here's an example from John who has experienced a

relationship breakdown

Statement *"I am feeling – angry"*

Why? *"Because Sarah dumped me"*

And this means that *"I'm unattractive to people"*

And this means that *"No one will want to be with me"*

And this means that *"I'm alone"*

And this means that *"I'm scared of being alone"*

Why? *"Because something may happen to me"*

And this means that *"I'll end up dying alone"*

And this means that *"I don't want to die alone"*

Why? *"Because I'm scared of dying"*

And this means that *"I don't want to die"*

You can see from the above example that several limiting beliefs have come to light

"I'm unattractive to people"

"I'm scared of being alone"

"I'm scared of dying"

Once you have your beliefs you can then go further by challenging them. You can do this by simply asking if your beliefs are true.

"I'm unattractive to people" Is that true? *"Well, I have had other relationships in the past and someone gave me their number the other day, so no, I guess it's not true"*

"I'm scared of being alone" Is that true? *"I spend a lot of my time alone at home and when I am driving my car to and from work I'm alone and I'm not scared, so no, I'm not scared of being alone"*

The previous life-limiting beliefs have fallen away as they are simply not true. The realization of this completely transmutes the energy around the belief, making it less dense and therefore more open to change. Once the belief is transmuted at the level of thought, any related imbalances on other levels of being also have the ability to change. If you are left with any statements that you believe are true then you can use the following techniques and see if they hold up to your enquiry. For example,

"I'm scared of dying" Is that true? *"Yes, I am scared of dying. I don't want my life to end."*

Why? *"Because I have so much left to do"*

And this means that *"I'll be cut off in my prime"*

Is this true? *"I don't know because I don't know when I'm going to die"*

And this means that *"I'm scared of not knowing"*

Why? *"Because I'm out of control of my life"*

The next step in your enquiry is to look for resonances on other levels of being. Ask yourself the following.

Where is the resonance? *"I feel it in my solar plexus"*

John has been shown a very clear signpost that is pointing to where the message is rooted in his system. He may also find that the imbalance manifests on one or more levels with physical or emotional feelings that accompany the message.

Resistance is futile, but fascinating!

"Vac Tapasya" is Sanskrit for *"speech penance"*. This exercise was developed by Brahmacharini Maya Tiwari, author of *"The Path of Practice"*. This exercise helps you to identify situations in your outer world that trigger negatively charged responses. By becoming aware of the triggers to our patterns we can gain greater understanding of ourselves.

In society there can be the pressure to come from a place of "love and light" at all times, especially within a spiritual community. This can create an unhealthy culture where feelings are not acknowledged because a person who is reacting negatively to a situation is perceived as being "bad" for expressing their feelings. Instead of suppressing or denying your thoughts and feelings this exercise helps you to transmute and process them.

Exercise: Vac Tapasya

Aim: The aim of this exercise is to identify inner resonances and offer them a vehicle for expression.

You will get most benefit from this exercise if you are open and honest with yourself so note down whatever negatively charged thoughts or emotions come up as you interact with your outside world. It could be while watching a television program or when having a conversation with a friend. No one need ever read what you have written so allow yourself the freedom of having a full-blown rant.

Here is an example where Alice writes about a meeting with her friend Jeanie.

I had coffee with Jeanie today and once again she was an absolute bitch to me. She is such a COW! She started off by making fun of the fact that I couldn't read the menu without my glasses and when I put them on called me *"spekky four eyes"* several times! She went on and on about her wonderful life, new job and fantastic boyfriend and made me feel so small. It's not fair, I'm still single and my job is *so* boring I could die. I'm on half the salary and am twice as smart, I'm sure she thinks I'm stupid. What the f***k is that all about???? I felt as though she was laughing at me behind my back. The final straw was when the gloating old hag offered to pay for the coffee as she'd just got a pay rise and she wanted to treat me. Bitch! She makes me feel so small, ugly and unattractive. I hate her! Hate her!

Once you have vented all of your feelings and thoughts read what you have written and reflect on what has shown up. We know that negative resonance is a reflection of your own inner condition. If there is no resonance, there is no issue. If Alice had no issues around the fact that she wears glasses then she would not even react to Jeanie's comments as there would be no resonance with her words. The reaction to the comments *"spekky four eyes"* could be attached to something around self-image or self-confidence. The chances are that Alice also has issues around her job. She mentions that it is *"so boring that I could die"* so why is she still in her job? Could there be a core message here that has resulted in a holding pattern? Perhaps she has fear around leaving her secure job. Even though it is boring she sees it as the *"devil she knows"* so she has chosen to stay on her energetic roundabout. Jeanie touched a nerve when she mentioned her new job as Alice wants the same thing and is very possibly angry with herself that she is unable, for whatever reason, to make the change.

Take full responsibility for the feelings at the root of your thoughts. Look back at what you have written during the Vac Tapasya exercise and where you say *"she, he or they"* change it to *"I"* and have another look at the statement. Is there a resonance with you on any level of your being? Be very honest with yourself. You are giving yourself a wonderful opportunity to move through your holding patterns.

No-one can make you do, feel, think or experience *anything*. If your boss repeatedly asks you to stay after work and you comply but complain to your family and colleagues, why are you doing that? It is your choice that you are feeling bad. Have a look at why you feel bad and work out the core message that is resonating with the experience. What is it that keeps you moaning about still being in the office after everyone has gone home?

If you are in a relationship with a person who is more dominant than you and they want to eat Indian food and you want to eat French, if you end up eating Indian food then this will be because you have chosen to allow their energy to entrain you. This only becomes an issue if you have a negatively charged reaction to the entrainment. For example, if you felt angry that you allowed yourself to be bullied by your partner which then reinforced the self-belief that you are weak, this is the message that you need to focus on during your sounding sessions. How often have you heard someone say *"you make me feel angry, sad, unloved, fat, stupid"* etc. This is simply not true. Not only is it untrue, it is impossible.

You can take this a step further by following *"The Work"*, which are four simple questions developed by Byron Katie. Her book, *"Loving What Is"* takes the reader through four simple questions which help identify the thoughts that are causing resistance and pain. Once identified, you can then turn the thoughts around and examine what comes up for you. Let's take the situation between Alice and Jeanie in the above example and use The Work to have a look at what is going on.

Statement – "Jeanie thinks I'm stupid"

Question 1 "Is it true?"

"Yes, it is true. She thinks that because I'm stuck in my old job that I must be stupid."

Question 2 "Can you absolutely know it is true?"

"Well, how can I know what she thinks, but I'm sure it is true. She's never actually told me that I'm stupid, so no; I don't have any proof that it is true."

Question 3 "How do you react, what happens, when you believe that thought?"

"I feel angry and tense. My stomach churns and I feel sick."

Question 4 "Who would you be without the thought?"

"I would be more confident, self-assured and relaxed. I would feel less stressed."

Then turn it around. The turnaround is an opportunity for you to look in the mirror and face what you are projecting. If you can, turn it around at least three times and explore what comes up. For example, *"Jeanie thinks I'm stupid"* can be turned around to *"Jeanie doesn't think I'm stupid"*, *"I think Jeanie is stupid"* and *"I think I'm stupid"*. Bingo! Everything you think about someone else, you really think about yourself. Interesting! According to Byron Katie *"until you see your enemy as your friend your work is not done"*. This is so true. The resistance that you feel is you telling yourself that you need further exploration in a certain area. Once you have realized that you have been believing a statement that is not true, you can then choose to let it go. Do you really want to hold on to such a life-limiting belief? You are helping yourself all the time, all you need to do is stop, listen and act.

I am not suggesting that we all go out and change our homes, jobs and relationships on a regular basis. One could argue that this wouldn't be healthy either and could be a sign of an under-lying pattern of another kind, perhaps the fear of commitment or being hurt, for example. If you are on an energetic roundabout that is draining you, ask yourself why.

"The harmony which the eye can see is not so mighty as that which cannot be seen"
Heraclitus

The Human Antenna Array

Human beings are an antenna array programmed to receive signals of all kinds. The brain decodes the plethora of frequencies we receive every second, makes sense of the input and sends it to the various centers that deal with that particular frequency. Our ears are auditory receptors programmed to receive frequencies between 16 and 20,000 Hz. Our eyes are visual receptors programmed to receive frequencies of 380 and 760 billion Hz. Our chakras also receive a variety of different frequencies depending on the nature and function of the chakra (we will be examining the chakras in more depth later on).

If there is a malfunction in the antenna array due to an imbalance of energy somewhere in your system you will be unable to receive the full range of frequencies available to you. This will undoubtedly have an impact on your health and wellbeing and to some extent your wings will be clipped. How much you are missing out on due to the limitations of your antennae will not be known until you begin the en-lightenment process. Only then will you begin to stretch your wings and reach for the stars.

In the previous chapter we looked at how your personal programs shape your reality. No computer will allow you to play the latest games without the appropriate software. It is the same with us. If we are running out-moded programs then even with the best intentions we will never be able to evolve.

In the film *"What the Bleep do we Know"* Dr Candace Pert tells the story of Columbus's first visit to the Americas. Every day the shaman of the village came down to the beach and looked out to sea. He could see a disturbance in the water but could not see the ships as his brain was unable to make sense of what he was seeing. After days and days of revisiting the shore line the ships began to appear. This interesting story has received much criticism regarding its validity and reliability. Whether this happened or not is not the issue, it is the concept that is worthy of discussion. One could argue that an infant seeing something for the first time does not have any concept of what they are seeing and therefore would their toys be hidden from sight? If this is the case, perhaps the input from the sense of touch helps to teach and support the visual receptors, allowing the object to be seen. Perhaps we come with a basic software program that enables us to make sense of basic objects, or maybe we download a "starter pack" from the various blueprints that exist in the mind of God.

In his book *"Musicophilia"*, Oliver Sacks includes an account of one of his patients who had been blind since birth. Following an eye operation at the age of fifty this patient had recovered limited sight. As his brain had not developed cognitive systems for making sense of what he was seeing he found tasks such as shaving extremely difficult because he found it hard to hold on to the image of his face in the mirror for more than a few moments before it became fragmented and unrecognizable. After persevering for some time he came to the realization that he did not have the software to support the new input his visual antenna was receiving and preferred to shave with his eyes closed instead. Many UFO enthusiasts believe that the ancient reports of people seeing dragons and flying boats were actually UFO's but due to the limitations of the onlookers' programs they used objects that were familiar to them (as well as myth and legend) to describe their experiences.

Dr Daniel Simons of the University of Illinois and Christopher Chabris of Harvard University worked together to produce a number of experiments which have become world famous. One of the most well-known is where an audience was asked to count the number of ball-passes made by a group of people playing basketball. During this activity a woman dressed in a gorilla suit walked slowly through the group and momentarily stopped in the middle to beat her chest in true gorilla fashion. Around half of the audience failed to notice the gorilla and did not believe that one had appeared during the game even though half of the group said they had seen it. When the video of the experiment was replayed everyone saw the gorilla walk through the basketball players. I have taken part in this exercise and I did not see the gorilla the first time because I was concentrating so hard on counting the passes made by the basketball players. It certainly raises the following questions. What are we looking at without *really* seeing and how much more of the world could become visible if we were able to open our minds? Does seeing enable us to believe or does believing help us to see?

As well as selective seeing we are also able to filter what we hear. How many teenagers develop selective hearing when asked to turn the TV off and do their homework or tidy their room? Have you ever "zoned out" of a conversation you are having when you hear a more interesting discussion going on somewhere else in the room?

On an emotional level people can become "hardened" to certain situations due to past traumas and heartbreak. There may well be events in your life that you are consciously or unconsciously choosing to filter out of your experience. In *"The Power of Sound"* Joshua Leeds shares his experience of blocking out the booming voice of his abusive father as a child. Not only could he not hear anyone else speaking in the same frequency range as his father clearly, he could not hear himself properly either. Following a course of sound therapy he was able to make a quantum shift, retuning his antenna and becoming more sensitive to the world. As a result his outer world changed and his relationship with his father also improved.

"enlightenment is an expanded form of perception dependent on neither ear nor eye that penetrates the deceptive filter our senses impose between ourselves and reality".

Joachim-Ernst Berendt

The En-Lightenment Process and the Garden of Eden

As you align to the mind of God your antenna array will receive a "tune up". Colors may seem more vibrant as you will be seeing them in their truer form due to the denser energy shifting from the visual antenna. Your hearing range may also increase and you may become more sensitive to certain sounds and the energy behind people's words. You may begin to see auras and energy fields and become more sensitive to the energy in your environment. Your intuition may also improve, allowing you to see your path ahead more clearly and make decisions more easily. Depending on your belief system you may begin to be aware of beings that inhabit other frequency ranges or dimensions such as guides and angels, the elemental world and extra-terrestrial beings.

Once thought of as being whacky and new age, the greatest scientific minds all over the world are crunching numbers in a race to prove the existence of the multi-verse. Although it has not yet been proven by science, I am in no doubt that the multi-verse exists. It is rather like tuning a radio. You can tune into one radio station and hear it perfectly. When you turn the dial slowly in any direction you may be able to hear another radio station "bleeding into" the original one before the next station becomes clear with a further tweak of the dial. Even though you are tuned into one radio frequency, you know that others are also broadcasting at the same time so the idea of beings in other dimensions is perfectly feasible.

To protect or not to protect

As you raise your consciousness you may become more aware of energies or beings in other realms. Tuning in to these beings is a matter of personal choice and one that can raise the question of protection. This is a subject which can challenge personal, cultural and religious beliefs.

In the early 1980's I joined a spiritual development group where it was regular practice to visualize the chakras opening before a session and closing at the end of the session. We also reinforced our protection by putting a bubble of light around the auric field. This felt right at the time and it was something I practiced for many years until I began to understand more about the nature of energy and explored the reasons why I felt the need to protect myself. This raised the question, what was I *actually* protecting myself from? Evil entities that were about to pounce on me any second? Was this *true?* When I examined my motivation for protecting myself further I realized that I was fearful of my own dark thoughts, my own shadow. Once I got to know my shadow and was able to dance happily with this aspect of myself I no longer needed protection.

Energy by its very nature is an ever changing, flowing and resonating field that feeds our antennae with information about our environment. When we examine the fundamental nature of energy do we *really* believe that it is possible to cut ourselves off from this flow by imagining that we are in a bubble and that our chakras are closed down? Saying that, intention is a very powerful force, so even though it is not possible to cut ourselves off from the mind of God completely, surely we are inhibiting our energy flow by thinking in this way? If you feel you are limiting your antenna array, examine the reasons why you are doing this as openly and honestly as possible. Ask yourself what is holding you back from achieving your fullest potential and use the exercises in this book to help you to move beyond the limits of your personal filters and holding patterns.

It is worth mentioning that not everyone experiences beings from other dimensions when they tune up their antenna array. It all depends on your personal software program and what frequencies you are comfortable with experiencing.

En-lightenment

The word "enlightenment" literally means "becoming lighter". Before you go rushing for the bathroom scales this lightness is not anatomically detectable but more of an energetic lightness (although some people I have worked with have lost physical weight due to working on the pattern which resulted in them overeating). This energetic lightness manifests as a feeling of wholeness. You look and feel complete and seem to radiate an outer glow. Thomas Ashley-Farrand, author of *"Healing Mantras"* shares a wonderful account of how a Buddhist visiting his home recognized that he chanted the Gayatri mantra by the glow that thousands of repetitions of this mantra had manifested within his auric field (the intention of the Gayatri mantra is to attain enlightenment and increases the amount of spiritual light in the system).

As you release denser energy and holding patterns from your system you will become en-lightened. Many people who are actively working with sound say that they look and feel younger and their body becomes more flexible. Enlightenment is also known as "moving into your light body", "expanding your energy", "ascending" and "shifting frequencies". The idea of a person being able to expand their energy has been criticized for being whacky, new age and even impossible. Let's examine this from a scientific perspective and then we can decide for ourselves.

Einstein's famous equation E=mc2 illustrated that matter is trapped light, the physicist David Bohm called matter *"frozen light"* and in her book *"Punk Science"* Dr Manjir Samanta-Laughton states that *"the underlying truth is that all is light"*. If matter is light being held in the physical form, then we *are* light. If we have become denser due to holding patterns and negatively charged energy then we could be seen as being "dimmer light"; rather like a dimmer switch being turned down. Therefore if we can release the holding patterns we will shine brighter and therefore will become "en-lightened".

In the past enlightenment was thought to be reserved for the purest of souls and holy men which, in my opinion, was a belief system put in place to dis-empower people so that they would look to others for answers and guidance. We no longer need to get answers from others because all of the answers, guidance and information we need is contained within the mind of God. Our human nature, ego and entrainment from outside influences cause us think we are separate from the mind of God which causes suffering. Remember Dr Fred Alan Wolf's particles of hate? In this case sometimes we need help and support from others to remind us that we are one, but at a deep level we *know* this and we *feel* the connection. So what has happened?

When one Became two

The story of Adam and Eve is typical of the programming that we receive that teaches us about separation. It is a story with a powerful message but I believe this message has been changed and misinterpreted over the years. The story of the Garden of Eden illustrates a time when people were one with God - there was no concept of separation. Once Eve allowed herself to be tempted by the apple she became conscious of herself as a separate entity which resulted in her and Adam being cast out of Eden. Surely the message is about separation rather than about humans disappointing God? Believing that we are separate from *anything* causes us pain and dis-ease. I believe we are still *in* the Garden of Eden; we never left. Eve didn't even pack her suitcase!

The illusion of separation is just that, an *illusion*. If we are all connected to the mind of God then how can we be separate? Even so, many of us are entrained to this belief which can set up fear patterns in the system resulting in fighting, control issues and a host of other negatively charged energy manifestations. To see the powerful force of entrainment at work all we have to do is open a newspaper or switch on the television.

Many of us *know* there is more to life and it is this inner knowing that has driven us to try anything and everything in order to make our way back to God; back to unity. It has driven us to walk on blazing embers, spend days in the desert, send people into space and build the Large Hadron Collider. Everything is a necessary part of our evolution and therefore everything is perfect. Our choice is whether or not to align to certain programs but the truth is we *are* God and God is us. It's that obvious you could trip over it.

The Silver Bowl

In the middle of a field sat a silver bowl full of water. One day a drop fell from the heavens and landed in the middle of the water, sending ripples to the edge. The energy of this falling drop caused each separate water drop that had ever fallen into the bowl to become conscious of itself. The drops started rushing towards the edge of the bowl, being carried on the energy of the ripples. Some of them hit the sides of the bowl and desperately clung to the edge, refusing to let go. They thought the sides were a place of refuge but this was the most chaotic place to be. The drops were buffeted here and there by currents but they clung on regardless feeling helpless, alone and in pain. Others felt that the center was the best place to be and headed for the source of the energy. As they let go of the sides they realized that it *was* less painful and tried to help the drops at the side of the bowl by telling them to let go and trust the energy of the ripples to carry them back to the center, but the drops at the side took no notice. Drops on the way back to the center met drops on the way to the edge and shared their experience of the chaos and pain at the sides of the bowl. Some drops on the way to edge took heed of this advice, turned around and headed straight for the center. Others felt that they needed to feel the pain at the side of the bowl just to see what it was like.

We are the water in the bowl. Some of us are under the illusion that we are separate beings with no connection. When you look at the ocean you do not see millions of separate drops, you see one body of water which ebbs and flows in unity. Looking at the water under a microscope you can see the individual molecules that the water is made from but you also know that these work perfectly together as a whole. This is the subject/object split that can cause confusion and pain, we *are* separate drops but we *are* also the whole.

Where are you in the silver bowl? Are you being buffeted by the chaos at the sides or are you heading towards the source? Wherever you are know that you have the power to change direction at any time.

According to the laws of sympathetic resonance and entrainment, we are also able to influence the drops in the silver bowl. The Global Coherence Initiative is a science-based initiative that aims to unite millions of people with the intention of helping to shift global consciousness. Different organizations and individuals have different calculations regarding how many people it would take to make a difference, but according to the GCI it only takes 5 per cent of the members of any organization to be able to create a shift in consciousness. As at July 2008 the world's population was approximately 6,706,993,152 people. Five percent of this number is 3.35 million, which is less than half of the population of London! If this number is correct it only takes a very small number of people to bring about a shift in consciousness within the collective.

Sound-workers also work to help raise planetary energy. Jonathan Goldman co-ordinates an initiative on the 14th February every year known as *"World Sound Healing Day"*. At an allotted time groups around the world tone "AH" (the tone of the heart chakra) with the intention of giving the Earth a sonic cuddle. At BAST we also run initiatives to send loving ripples through the silver bowl. The last one was an hour's chanting of "Om Shanti" (supreme peace) on International World Peace Day. If this idea resonates with you I encourage you to join the existing initiatives and/or form your own groups. Everything helps.

It is interesting that after thousands of years of entraining influences some of us are more comfortable with the idea of being separate than we are of being connected. When I give talks which touch on the illusion of separation I am sometimes met with resistance. If you feel resistance to the idea of being connected to all that is, I encourage you to embrace and explore this resistance through the exercises in this book. In the next chapter we will explore the illusion of separation further and say hello to the aspect of ourselves that likes to get involved called "the ego".

"Our respective tribes introduce us to life 'in the world'. They teach us that the world is either safe or dangerous, abundant or poverty-ridden, educated or ignorant, a place to take from or to give to."
Caroline Myss

Tribal Patterning and the Ego

An ego is something which has a boundary, and therefore a container of some sort. Tribal ego was perhaps the first ego to exist. Individuals were either inside or outside the tribe and therefore were the same as, or separate from, the group. Any group can be considered a tribe, including religious groups, sporting teams and their faithful supporters, families, cultures, races and political groups. Any group that unites people together in an identifiable way is a tribe. Jung considered the group mind to be the lowest form of consciousness and felt that members that became engaged in negatively charged activities within the group rarely accepted responsibility for their role and actions. You may be familiar with the term "safety in numbers". It is as if the group protects the individual in some way. You can see this happen when political party spin doctors rally round when a leader or party member makes a *faux-pas*. In *"Anatomy of the Spirit"*, Caroline Myss states that *"once we accept responsibility for even one area of our lives, we can never again use tribal reasoning to excuse our behavior"*.

If a tribe attempts to create a distance between itself and others this can cause the energy of the group to begin to come from a place of power rather than unity and love. Through the entrainment principle we know that the collective energy of a group is far more powerful than an individual and that large numbers of people can become entrained without fully realizing what is happening. Adolf Hitler was a very powerful entraining force and the leader of a tribe that attempted to take over a large part of the world.

Coming from the place of power means that the energy has

"descended" from the unconditional level of the heart center to the base and solar plexus chakras (interestingly, Carolyne Myss calls the base chakra the *"tribal chakra"*). I believe that many of the wars on this planet are created by tribal ego. On one hand, being part of a tribe can create a sense of belonging and safety and on the other hand it is reinforcing separation, which our higher self perceives as an unnatural state of being. Our energy starts doing the *"particle boogie"* which causes suffering and pain. This suffering and pain is projected out into the world as war, violence, hatred, discrimination and so on.

People gain love, support and comfort from groups and one could argue that they can reinforce the feeling of unity and unconditional love. However by its nature a group makes a clear definition between those who belong and those who do not and therefore has an ego. I am not suggesting that you cancel your membership to your local wine club or spiritual development group but awareness of where you are coming from when you are part of your group and how this influences you is important. Do you feel negatively entrained by your tribe? In *"Anatomy of the Spirit"* Caroline Myss also links illness to imbalances within the tribe. She uses the example of the polio epidemic which occurred in the USA in the 1930's and 1940's. In Myss' opinion the stress of the Great Depression caused people to feel they were being "crippled" by the economic crash. Shortly following the crash a polio epidemic took hold leaving many people physically, as well as emotionally and/or financially crippled. At the time of writing this book the world is being gripped by the "Global Credit Crunch". The world's press is drawing comparisons between this and the Great Depression and so it will be really interesting to see if the health of the world is affected by the energy of this event.

Energetic boxes

In *"Matter into Feeling"* Dr Fred Alan Wolf states that when a particle has a defined boundary it acts like a wave, spreading out to fit the container it is in. The ego is a container; our physical body is a container in fact the universe is *full* of energy containers. If we think about it our limiting beliefs and symptoms are also containers as they limit our ability on some level. Energetically, particles in smaller containers have denser patterns and are more resistant to change. They also require more energy to change and when change happens it is usually in the form of large, erratic changes in state, rather than the smaller gradual changes of energy in a pattern that is less dense.

Wolf states that *"an electron free to roam in a box as big as a room would constantly undergo miniscule energy changes"*. Therefore the more flexible your energy is the easier you are able to accept change and the less likely you are to react strongly to changes that occur in your life. You can *"go with the flow"*.

You know when you have enabled an energy container to become larger when you experience a process or reaction following the energy work you are doing. A sounding session may bring "stuff" up for you to a greater or lesser degree. Depending on the level that the imbalance was on this can be a physical, emotional, mental or spiritual process (or a combination of these). We know that it takes more energy to produce changes in a denser holding pattern, but sometimes the energy shifts dramatically. A healing crisis occurs when a person experiences a dramatic change due to their energy suddenly springing to another state of potential. It is important to recognize when this is happening and meet your needs accordingly. Take things easy, look after yourself and don't try to push yourself with further exploration and treatments of different kinds. Allow your system to assimilate the new energy potential but keep moving towards your new way of being. That is, don't allow yourself to snap back into the old container move into your new expanded container gently and enjoy the space it gives you.

Harry the Hermit crab needs a new home. His old shell is chafing and clearly doesn't fit anymore. He is going to have to move but he is scared because he could run the risk of being snapped up by a predator, but it has become too painful to stay. Once in his new home he'll feel vulnerable until he grows into the space but after a short time he will be able to stretch out and enjoy his newly-found freedom.

It is normal to feel fear and resistance to change, but if we consider the nature of energy we know that change is the only constant, this is a given. If you are resisting the changes that you instinctively know that you need, it could be because there is a core message underneath which is fear-based. Next time you feel the pull to retreat into your old shell, follow Harry's example and go and find a new one.

It can take time to adjust to change, especially if the holding pattern you are transmuting is dense. It is rather like receiving a treatment from an osteopath when something has been out of alignment for a long time. The osteopath makes their adjustment and you come out feeling a little sore but better. After a while the muscles that may have been programmed over many years are unable to transcend their pattern after one treatment so they begin to pull your back out again. After the next visit to the osteopath you are less sore and your back stays better for longer. The more you relax your muscles and make the changes to your lifestyle and posture, the better you feel. The new pain-free you is now able to explore new and exciting areas in your life. Think of this work as energetic osteopathy, the more flexible you become, the more you will be able to achieve.

"Not only is there an overwhelming probability that the entropy of a physical system will be higher in what we call the future, but there is the same overwhelming probability that it was higher in what we call the past."

Brian Greene

Youthing, Loving, Age-ing and Sage-ing

We know that we are trapped light. When matter emits energy it loses some of its light and therefore some of its "self". Our sun is a good example. It is a large, bright source of light. It warms our faces, enables our crops to grow and without it all life on Earth would cease. As the sun shines it ages; loosing 14 million tons of mass every second. Everything loses mass as it ages. We may begin to shrink in height; our bones may become more brittle and our skin drier. Our tendons shorten, causing tension and contraction in the joints and we can be prone to constipation, dry eyes and mouth. All of these symptoms are due to a loss of energy or light. As we age we lose light, our energy containers become more contracted and as a result the energy within them becomes denser.

This loss of light is not just confined to the physical level. People sometimes use the expression "they are set in their ways" to describe a person whose behavior is constricted. We may like to take our holidays in the same place, eat the same meals, visit the same places and shop in the same stores. We can fall into a rut (remember the energetic roundabouts?). One could argue that as we get older we know what we like and what works for us and this is fine, but if you are sitting on the same beach for the fifth year running and secretly wishing you were somewhere else what are you doing? Top up your light and get out there!

The aging process is known in physics as *"entropy"*. Understanding this fundamental law is paramount when helping to stay young on all levels. In his book, *"Physics of the Soul"* Dr.Amit Goswami states that *"entropy produces wear and tear in the physical body which is the hardware for creativity to make new programmes that we call learning. Eventually entropy wins this battle and the organism ceases to evolve itself with further creativity. This is when consciousness begins to withdraw. This withdrawal terminates in death."* If you can identify the areas of withdrawal, contraction and shrinkage in your life and adopt energy expanding exercises you will keep your system topped up with light, allowing creativity to flow and therefore you will stay younger and more flexible for longer. I have observed people becoming more physically, emotionally and mentally flexible since they began working with sound and other light increasing exercises.

In her book "In Resonance", Jasmuheen states that *"the higher the quotient of light within the body, the stronger our natural ability for cellular regeneration on the purest level"*. We know that the photon is the light emitting *"love particle"*, therefore if we increase the love in our life we also increase the light.

But we *know* that we age. This is a Newtonian viewpoint of cause and effect, with the physical body moving from young to old along the linear illusion of time but according to the nature of energy at the quantum level, the Newtonian laws of cause, effect and linear time simply don't exist. Therefore is it possible that we can *"youth"* rather than age? I believe the key to the fountain of youth is our intention as it is our belief that shapes our reality. If you align yourself to the belief that you can stay younger for longer then there is no reason why you cannot live a longer and healthier life.

Aligning to bliss

Many people working with the techniques in this book tell me that they become more able to deal with certain aspects of their lives that they previously found difficult. This certainly has been my experience. Since I began working with sound I have been able to achieve and sustain a deep level of connection and unconditional love. As a result I now find that issues which previously caused me stress and worry do not resonate with me. I still experience resonances in my system, but I now have a greater awareness around why they are there and the gifts of learning that they bring. With sound and self-awareness exercises I am able to transmute the energy around my resistances easily and effectively.

We know that we only experience negatively charged emotions when there is something within for the feelings to resonate with. If you are resonating with the frequency of love and bliss, you have more light in your system and therefore denser negatively charged energy is transmuted before it has the chance to manifest on the levels of your being.

As you have been working with the en-lightenment exercises in this book you may have found that the "new" you does not resonate with your "old" life and that you are being confronted with choices. Do you stay in the old life or allow yourself to open to another potential, one that feeds your soul and allows you to live in love and bliss. Living in bliss is a result of aligning to the mind of God but does not mean being unable to function in the real world. It means being grounded and fully present in the moment and free of negative entrainment. It enables you to come from a loving core when communicating with others.

"The human brain is an enchanted loom where millions of flashing shuttles weave a dissolving pattern, always a meaningful pattern, though never an abiding one, a shifting harmony of sub-patterns. It is as if the Milky Way entered upon some cosmic dance."

Sir Charles Sherringham

The Human Brain

The patterns made by groups of neurons are known as brain-waves. This electrical activity in the brain is measured by an electroencephalogram (EEG). We are discovering more about the human brain all the time and advancements in brainwave technology have shown us that several different brainwave frequencies can be hidden or "folded" within others, allowing the brain to be in several different states at the same time. Even though the brain will be running concurrent frequencies there will be a frequency that predominates.

It is well-known that sound and music helps the brain to achieve relaxing states as well as those of heightened awareness. Even inexperienced meditators find it much easier to achieve deeper states when working with sound. The gentle tones or repetition of a rhythm entrains the brainwaves into a more relaxed way of being, distracting it from the chatter that many people are challenged with during other meditation techniques.

To enable entrainment to take place it is ideal to avoid too much interference in the sound frequencies by playing too loudly, with too much melody and/or in an erratic manner. If you do this you may find that the brain will shift out of a relaxed state into a higher, more alert state. A little understanding of the different brainwave frequencies and their effects will help you to construct your wholing sessions more effectively.

Epsilon less than 0.5 Hz Suspended animation

This brainwave frequency is a fairly new discovery. It is the state that Yogi's achieve when they place themselves in suspended animation where their pulse is almost undetectable. They enter this state to increase the flow of prana and claim it increases longevity. Perhaps this state also helps activate the flow of nectar through the Bindu Visharga, allowing the practitioner to "live on light".

(see the chapter on the Chakras for more information on the Bindu Visharga).

Delta 0.5-3 Hz Sleep:

Delta waves are slow, large waves. A person in this brainwave state will be in a deep and dreamless sleep. Two-thirds of your time asleep is devoted to your brain being in delta as the body uses this state to repair itself from the day's activities and give the brain time to rest.

Theta 3-7 Hz Reverie, imagery, near sleep:

This brainwave state occurs in light sleep. An indication of the brain being predominantly in Theta is rapid eye movement (REM), dreams, and hallucinations. The brain uses this state to exercise itself and to release tension. Mental imagery and psychic experiences can occur in Theta. Your brain cells also reset their sodium/potassium ratios in this frequency. If you have spent a long time in a higher frequency such as Beta the ratio between the potassium and sodium in your system is out of balance, which can contribute to mental fatigue and "burnout". Five to fifteen minutes in Theta can restore this ratio to normal, resulting in mental refreshment.

Alpha-Theta border 7-8 Hz Creativity, intelligence.

Too much sensory input caused by stress, shock or damage to the physical body can cause overload. In this state the central nervous system reduces input from the peripheral nervous system. Without these systems to control the brain expands its functioning powers and the lesser used parts of the brain become active. It is interesting to note the correlation between this frequency and the resonant frequency of the Earth, which is one of the reasons why we consider 8hz to be one of the *"optimum wholing frequencies"*. When you are in this state you are conscious of all things around you and yet the body and mind are in deep relaxation.

Alpha 8-12 Hz Relaxed

This wave is slightly faster than Theta and is associated with ESP and meditation. This state occurs during relaxation, usually with the eyes closed, as well as when you are day dreaming and when you are in deep reflection, such as when you are checking for resonance in the system.

Beta 13-30 Hz Awake and alert

Beta is associated with the fully conscious and focused mind. Stimulants such as caffeine and nicotine can artificially induce this state. High Beta waves without Alpha is associated with stress, anxiety and high blood pressure so if you are under stress it is vital that you manage this with lower frequency brainwave states to avoid mental fatigue and a host of other stress related symptoms.

Gamma 30 - 56 Hz Hyperawareness

Research has shown that during bursts of precognition or when high-level information is being processed your brainwaves briefly reach the Gamma state. This brainwave activity is associated with states of self awareness, higher levels of insight and information, psychic abilities and out of body experiences. This frequency is also thought to be the "binding or harmonizing" frequency, allowing for experiences such as seeing, hearing and feeling to be bound together as one experience.

Hyper-Gamma 100Hz & Lambda 200Hz

These frequencies are to be found during deep meditation and higher levels of cognition. When a certain sect of Tibetan monks was studied during their meditations there were times when their brainwaves reached these higher frequencies. To demonstrate the power of meditation the monks, many of them wearing little more than a loin-cloth, sit in the snow in sub-zero temperatures and allow wet towels to be placed on their shoulders. This would quickly induce hyperthermia in most people, but by achieving a deep state of meditation they are able to generate enough body heat to make the towels steam and melt the snow around them.

It is interesting that the Epsilon frequency is also associated with very similar states of being. With the advancement of brainwave research it has been found that these frequencies co-exist. According to Beth Coleman, *"the Hyper-Gamma, Lambda and Epsilon frequencies are linked together in a circular relationship"* she goes on to say that when the brain exhibits the higher frequencies, you will also find Epsilon folded into the frequency and vice-versa. This interesting relationship is one that requires further investigation. During the sounding exercises in Part II of this book your brainwaves may well slow to between 3 and 12 hz and there may even be times when Epsilon, Gamma and Hyper-Gamma frequencies are present, especially if you are experiencing bursts of pre-cognition.

"... a new language, a sign and formula of which mathematics and music equally partake, enabling one to combine astronomical and musical formulas, a common denominator for mathematics and music. The law of the octave is this principle where mathematics and music equally partake. This law makes it possible to combine astronomical and musical formulas. It is the common denominator of astronomy, mathematics, music and color"

Herman Hesse

The Law of the Octave

The word octave means "of eight". An octave in western music is taken from one point in the major scale to the same point one octave higher so, C3 to C4 on a piano is one octave. The law of the octave is a mathematical law that connects us to all things. If this law is applied frequencies that were previously out of our hearing range can be heard. By using a simple process of multiplication or division (depending on whether you want a higher or lower octave) it is possible to hear the vibrations of the planets, buildings and even our DNA. An interesting inscription was found in an abbey in Cluny, France. It reads *"the Octave teaches the saints bliss"*. Through the law of the octave, the soundworker can form a relationship with any entity, be it an object, color or vibration.

Pythagoras called the subtle sounds coming from the heavenly bodies *"The Music of the Spheres"* and, according to the Pythagorean tradition, only he could hear these heavenly tones. He calculated the intervals between the planets by using the Earth as the baseline, creating the "Pythagorean Scale" which is C, D, D#, E, G, A, A#, B, D. Pythagoreans believed that these heavenly tones had a profound effect on our overall health and well-being. Inspired by the work of Pythagoras, the musicologist and mathematician Hans Cousto has taken this to another level in his book *"The Cosmic Octave"*.

The octave is usually the first musical interval to be taught with regard to harmony and the first harmonic of the harmonic series. Compared to all the other musical intervals the octave creates the strongest resonance which is the reason why its laws are applied to all resonating objects. I have included a number of correspondences in this book, but I have only skimmed the surface. If you are interested in the law of the octave I encourage you to look deeper. Here are a few correspondences to whet your appetite.

The Earth's auric field is known as the Schumann Cavity. Lightening strikes and electro-magnetic impulses all have an effect on this cavity, creating an overall fundamental frequency of 7.83hz which is known as the "Schumann Resonance". Interestingly, it is almost exactly the same as an octave of the Earth year which is 8.5hz (C#). When we are in a relaxed and harmonious state, our brainwave pattern is Alpha, which is the frequency of the Earth year. It is also no surprise to note that the frequency of OM (the sound of creation) is C#. Warren J Hammerman's research showed that the human body resonates at a frequency of 570 trillion hertz which is 42 octaves above middle C. Fritz Popp discovered that human DNA resonated at a frequency of 854 trillion hertz, which is the 66th octave of the Earth day (G). When C and G are played together they create a perfect fifth which interestingly is the musical interval that humans find most harmonious as well as being the interval that the human body conforms to.

I never fail to be humbled and amazed each time I delve deeper into the law of the octave but, when you think about it, it makes perfect sense. We have evolved within the energy field of mother Earth and therefore it is no surprise that we are resonating with her song. We are octaves of her blueprint, harmonic chips off the old block!

Sound, color and shape
The color spectrum is approximately forty octaves above the

hearing spectrum. If it were possible to tune a piano up by forty octaves, theoretically it would play color instead of sound. When I am conducting a therapeutic sound session my clients and/or workshop participants often tell me that they saw color whilst the sound was interacting with their system. You may also experience colors during your sounding sessions. I believe there are several reasons why this happens. It could be that you are sensing the color of the sound at an energetic level; you could be perceiving the colors of your own auric field; you could be drawing on a color frequency that you need at this time, or you could be a synaesthete.

Synaesthesia is labeled as a neurological condition although many synaesthetes consider it to be a gift. One in ten people are considered to have this ability. There are centers within the brain which are dedicated to speech, sound, taste, sensation and sight. It is thought that somewhere within the brain the synapses between these centers become cross-wired, sending information to a different center than the one that should be receiving the signal. Richard Cytowic gives many examples of synaesthesia in his book, *"The Man Who Tasted Shapes"*. These examples include a woman who saw a bird singing and at the same time as hearing the sound she was seeing blue bubbles coming from the bird's beak.

If you perceive sound as color, taste, shape or physical sensation it could be that you are a synaesthete. Many of the world's greatest composers and artists, poets were synaesthetes but synaesthesia is not only confined to people with an artistic nature. A psychological experiment designed by Woolfgang Kohler demonstrated that most of us have synaesthesic tendencies. Kohler asked people to choose which of the shapes overleaf would be named "Booba" and which was "Kiki". As many as 98 per cent of everyone asked chose Kiki for the angular shape and Booba for the rounded shape. This could be because Booba is a round sound when spoken and the "k" in Kiki sounds sharp. What do you think?

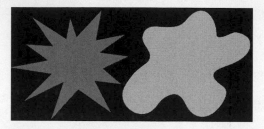

Which one is Booba and which is Kiki and why?

"The chakras represent the places of the physical body where representations (the organs) are made of vital body blueprints for biological form making, or morphogenesis."

Amit Goswami

Chakras and Nadis
The Wheels and Channels of Life

The first accounts of the chakra system appeared in the Vedic texts over four thousand years ago. The word *"chakra"* is the Sanskrit for *"wheel"*. The chakras were seen as spinning vortexes of energy situated mainly in the spinal column. Their function is to transfer energy or prana throughout the body via the "nadis" meaning "channels" or "currents". The Nadis are similar to the meridians in the traditional system of Chinese medicine. Our chakras transfer energy between our levels of being and the mind of God. Traditionally the chakras were described as spinning colored wheels or lotus flowers and over thousands of year's deities, Yantras (geometric shapes), animals, body parts, symbols, emotions, shapes, colors and of course sounds have been attributed to each of the chakras.

Different systems work with a different number of chakras, some of which are considered as major and some as minor. In the BAST method of sound therapy we work with ten chakras, but feel free to work with as many or few as you like. It is important that you find a system that resonates with you. Each of the chakras is situated along the mid-line of the body from base to crown. There are also chakras in the palms of the hands and soles of the feet but these are not included in the ten we will be working with although you may feel them being activated during a sounding session. The chakras in the soles of the feet connect us with Mother Earth. In the Bible there are accounts of people bathing Jesus' feet and being healed. Some say that this was due to the energy coming from the chakras in the soles of the feet. Hands-on healers channel energy from the universal source through their palm chakras to the part of the body they are working on.

Just as we can hold denser energy on the different levels of being, energy can also be held within the chakras. As you transmute denser energy from your system and expand your energy containers you may find that anything held in the chakras is also transmuted, allowing them to grow and develop. Some say that as we evolve more chakras will eventually be awakened and will join to create one central energy channel. In the years I have been working with sound I have experienced more chakras making themselves known so perhaps this is the case. Or perhaps they were always there but as I have transmuted the energy in my system they have come to light, rather like fog being evaporated by the sun to reveal more of the landscape.

On the physical level it is interesting to note the correlation between chakras and nerve plexuses. There are places in the body where the nerves combine to form plexuses (large masses) which relate to the skin, bones, muscles and joints of a particular area. There are five major nerve plexuses found on either side of the spinal column which are the Coccygeal, Sacral, Solar, Cardiac, Brachial, and Cervical. Some of these plexuses are close to the site of the chakras. According to Vedic medicine, the energy that is collected by the chakras is converted and sent to the body's systems via the endocrine system and the nervous system.

The endocrine system is one of the body's main physical control mechanisms. It comprises a number of ductless glands that are responsible for the production of many different hormones such as adrenaline, insulin, oestrogen and progesterone. These are secreted into the bloodstream to stimulate or inhibit certain physical processes. The endocrine system, along with the autonomic nervous system, helps maintain the parameters needed for optimum health. The chakra, nervous and endocrine systems are connected and therefore an imbalance in one area could lead to dis-ease in another.

The chakras are part of our antenna array. Each one filters our experience in a different way depending on its function. A healthy chakra will process the information it receives efficiently and without issue but an imbalanced chakra will not be able to do its job to the best of its ability. As the energy in the chakra continues to get denser, it could result in neighboring chakras becoming overworked and stressed as they will be trying to compensate for the imbalance. If the energy imbalance continues to increase in density it will begin to filter through the other levels of being until it eventually manifests in dis-ease. This is why it is good to check for resonances in the chakra system. We know that the resonances can be positively or negatively charged and because we are only looking for destructive and draining energy we are therefore concentrating on the negatively charged resonances in the system as these are pointing to a chakra that is having difficulty in processing the information it is receiving from the environment due to denser energy in that area.

The following correspondences are intended to give you an idea of the energy of each of the chakras. I have purposely avoided making too many emotional correspondences as the same emotions can be experienced through the filters of different chakras. For example, you can experience anger as a result of being physically threatened (base chakra), feeling out of control (solar plexus) or being unable to communicate (throat chakra). Feeling anger as a result of being unable to communicate could resonate with a memory around being beaten as a child, for example, and therefore could resonate in the base chakra but may also affect the throat.

During your alignment and sounding sessions it is likely that certain chakras will resonate. You may also find that this happens as you interact with your world. The information you receive from your chakras during your sessions will give you a good idea about the nature of the imbalance and the more you use the exercises in this book, the more you will be able to detect even the most subtle energy changes in your system. Remember there is no right or wrong. If you concentrate a sounding session on your throat chakra and the imbalance is rooted in the base chakra it doesn't matter as denser energy will still be transmuted and you will be topping up your light. You may find that in your next session you are guided to the base chakra due to the clarity you have gained resulting from your last session.

If you require more information on the chakras and their correspondences you can always refer to Liz Simpson's *"Book of Chakra Healing"*, *"Theories of the Chakras"* by Hiroshi Motoyama, *"Wheels of Light"* or *"Eastern Body and Western Mind"* which are both by Anodea Judith and *"Chakras and Nadis"*, by Swami Atmananda. I have drawn from all of these sources to compile the following list of correspondences as well as contributed my own findings. I have also given a longer description of the Bindu Visharga as I believe that this is a fascinating and underestimated center that is worth exploring in more depth.

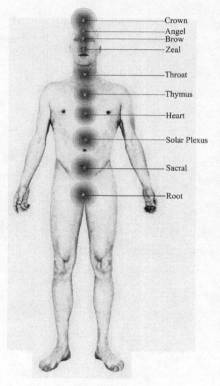

Crown
Angel
Brow
Zeal
Throat
Thymus
Heart
Solar Plexus
Sacral
Root

The Chakras

Base (Muladhara) Note C

Physical level – On the physical level this chakra corresponds with our skeletal structure, legs, gonads, adrenal glands and the base of the spine. The adrenal glands also produce adrenaline, the hormone for our "fight or flight" response. The base chakra is associated with physical survival and our physical identity. The adrenal glands also secrete a variety of hormones including those that regulate the body's metabolism of fats, proteins and carbohydrates as well as releasing hormones that help to balance the amount of salt in our bodily fluids.

Emotional level – The emotional correspondences for this chakra are fear and fearlessness bordering on recklessness and complete disregard for physical safety.

Mental Level – This chakra is related to our thoughts around the physical body and physical survival. An imbalance in this center can manifest in a range of emotions that one could display as a result of feeling physically threatened such as anger, fear and panic.

Spiritual level – This chakra is connected to the collective tribal consciousness and our connection with the earth energy.

Sacral (Svadisthana) Note D

Physical level – This chakra is located approximately two finger-widths below the naval and corresponds to the element of water, bladder, spleen, prostate and womb. It is also related to the movement and flexibility of the body and can be connected with lower back and hip pain and stiffness.

Emotional level – This chakra is related to the emotions that are associated with sex and sexuality, emotional intelligence and pleasure.

Mental level – Limiting thoughts, belief systems and core messages connected with sexuality, flexibility and reproduction are associated with this chakra. Do you go with the flow in life? Do you think you deserve pleasure?

Spiritual Level – This chakra is related to allowing the universal flow of energy and experiencing spiritual bliss and connection. It is also to do with the relationship we have with the mind of God.

Solar Plexus (Manipura) Note E

Physical level – This chakra is located between the navel and the heart. It is related to the digestive system, muscles, pancreas and liver. One of the physical imbalances of this chakra is diabetes. Anatomically the adrenal glands are located closer to the solar plexus than the base chakra which is one of the reasons why we experience butterflies in the stomach when we are nervous or feel out of control. It also could account for the connection that these two chakras share with regard to tribal ego. The solar plexus chakra is related to the element of fire – hence the term "fire in the belly".

Emotional level - This chakra is known as the "power center" and is related to the will and the need to control and be controlled. Any imbalances that are connected with control issues and personal power could resonate in this center.

Mental level – The solar plexus chakra is associated with any thoughts, beliefs and holding patterns associated with personal power, control, manipulation, self esteem, anxiety and perfectionism.

Spiritual level – This chakra is related to the power of the spirit within and without. Feeling out of control of your own destiny and out of touch with your path ahead is a characteristic of an imbalance in this center. Also feeling overwhelmed by or fearful of your own spiritual energy and wanting to control it, or wanting to control spiritual energy from other sources. By letting go of attachment and transcending the illusion of the ego-self one is able to transform energy held at this chakra.

Heart (Anahata) Note F

Physical level – This chakra is related to the air element and therefore is connected with the breath. Physical imbalances within this chakra can manifest as disorders of the heart, circulation, lungs, chest, blood pressure and mid back. Thymus imbalances can also be related to this chakra.

Emotional level – Emotions around loving and being loved unconditionally, relationships, empathy, joy, jealousy, the repression and expression of grief and coping with loss often resonate in this chakra.

Mental level – Any thoughts or belief systems we may have around unconditional love, giving and receiving and judgments that we make about others and ourselves can be connected to the heart chakra. Self-love, letting go, allowing people into your heart and expression of the energy of the heart are also related.

Spiritual level – This chakra is related to the blissful realization of the connectedness of all things as well as giving and receiving divine love and seeing divine love in all things.

Thymus (no Sanskrit name found as yet) Note F#

Physical level – This chakra is related to the thymus and the immune system. There are also physical connections with the throat and heart. This center can also be linked to growth, especially in early life. It also has a purifying role in the body by stimulating the production of lymphocytes which form part of our defense system, attacking invading organisms and providing immunity. This chakra is related to transitions and if you choose to manifest an illness to enable you to change your life, then this could be related to the thymus chakra.

Emotional level – This chakra is related to serenity, peacefulness and balanced emotions. If we find ourselves continually expressing our pain to others this can point to an imbalance in the thymus chakra. A balanced thymus enables us to be emotionally objective.

Mental level – Any thoughts, beliefs and core messages you have around blaming yourself or others can resonate in this chakra as can the inability to make decisions of the heart or take responsibility for your thoughts. It is also linked to integrity. If your thoughts become fixed and are unable to evolve easily this could indicate an imbalance in this chakra.

Spiritual level – This is the center where the choice is made whether or not the divine unconditional love of the heart is communicated without judgment both verbally and through our actions. In my opinion, light-workers need to focus extra attention on this center as well as the heart when they are channeling the mind of God to others through teaching, hands on healing or other means of communication. The ego can tend to cause the energy to come from the base and/or solar plexus. If you feel this happening, focus your attention and intention on the heart and thymus.

Throat (Vishuddha) Note G

Physical level – This chakra is found at the base of the throat. It is related to sound and linked to the thyroid and parathyroid, neck, physical development, mouth, ears and throat. The thyroid gland manufactures thyroxin which controls the body's metabolic rate. Behind this lies the parathyroid gland which controls the level of calcium in the bloodstream. A weak or overpowering voice can also indicate an imbalance in this center.

Emotional level – Any feelings you have around expressing your identity can indicate an imbalance in this chakra as well as difficulty with putting feelings into words. Emotions that have to do with the inability to express yourself creatively; listening to yourself and others and hearing and speaking the truth may also resonate here.

Mental level – This chakra is connected to mental development. It is also related to thoughts as well as patterns and belief systems you may have around personal communication, your personal identity and the ability to think creatively. Compulsive lying can also indicate an imbalance in this center.

Spiritual level – The elemental correspondence for the throat is ether. The throat chakra is also connected with sound vibrations as well as creative spiritual energy. It is at this level that we verbalize our intention.

Zeal Point (Bindu Visharga) Note G#

The Bindu (meaning point) features in certain important yantras (sacred power symbols) such as the Sri Yantra. The dot in the center of this powerful yantra symbolizes the creative point of the universe, the point of origin and return, the unity of male and female. The Zeal point is the representation of this point within the human body. According to traditional teachings, when you awaken the bindu visharga you hear the creation sound of OM. This is true alignment to the mind of God.

Physical level – If you run your fingers down the back of the skull you can feel a slight dip and then a raised area. This is the bindu visharga. Krishna devotees tie a ponytail at this point to remind them of the connection that this center has to the creator. Cranial nerves stem from this area including nerves that are connected to the eyes. This chakra is also related to the back of the head, sinuses, nose, throat (as a secondary center), ears and brain. It is linked to time and timelessness and the physical perception of time.

Emotional level – this chakra is related to any emotions concerning the unity of all things, where we come from and our belonging and connection to all that is. It is also connected to emotions around the passage of time, past, present and future.

Mental level – Hallucinations and psychotic episodes could be connected with an imbalance in this center as well as our thoughts and beliefs around the mind of God and the divine realms. Our thoughts around spiritual belief systems and where we come from correspond to this chakra.

Spiritual level - Certain energy expanding techniques can stimulate the production of a substance referred to as "nectar" which is collected at this center and when cultivated and channeled can allow a person to achieve superhuman feats. Yogis claim to have survived without food, water or air for very long periods of time. Some have reported being buried for as many as forty days. Swami Atmananda, the author of *"Chakras and Nadis"* states that *"the Bindu is the gateway to the infinite void where zero and infinity, nothingness and fullness exist simultaneously"*. It was traditionally thought that spiritual energy first enters through the bindu visharga before manifesting the myriad of objects that form our experience.

Brow (Ajna) Note A

Physical level – This chakra is also known as the 'third eye'. It is related to the pituitary gland and is located between the eyebrows. It is also linked to the hypothalamus, pituitary, eyes, base of skull, autonomous nervous system. It is related to the element of light.

Emotional level – Any emotions there may be around the inability to make sense of what you are seeing and of your path ahead can be held in this chakra. If you are unable to feel what you see it could be because of an imbalance in this center.

Mental level – This chakra can be linked to escapism, fantasy and preferring to live in an imaginary world as well as obsessive thoughts, difficulty in concentrating and lack of imagination.

Spiritual level - This chakra is related to light, archetypal identity, intuition, wisdom, visualization, and clairvoyance. When balanced it allows us to see by enhancing our psychic perception and allowing us to see the "bigger picture".

Angel (no known Sanskrit name found as yet) Note A#

Some years ago I began to notice another center appearing when scanning the chakras and some of the students at BAST also confirmed this. Shortly after this chakra made its first appearance one of my students came into college with an article that she had found in the *"Sunday Times"* referring to the lowest sound in the universe. This sound was detected in September 2003 and seemed to be coming from a super massive black hole in the Perseus galaxy 250 million light-years from Earth. The note was an A# that was 57 octaves below middle C and is the deepest sound so far detected. Could it be that on some level our energy systems were resonating with this sound, facilitating the awakening of this center or was this center always present but was undetected until recently?

Physical level – This chakra is related to the pineal and pituitary glands, the eyes, head, autonomous nervous system and light. In *"The Tantra of Sound"* Jonathan Goldman shares an experience he had in a Mayan temple in Palenque when he and a group of people witnessed light being created by toning a sound that created light. This was a wonderful experience and can be an energetic shift. This can also happen when the sound stimulates the optic nerve, especially when you are toning sounds that resonate with the Zeal Point, Brow, Angel and Crown chakras.

Emotional level – This center is associated with the emotions which are related to both the brow and the crown chakras.

Mental level – This chakra has connections with the thoughts we have around transcending our experiences beyond the physical body into our light bodies. Any resistance to this process could resonate in this chakra.

Spiritual level – The Angel chakra is related to the creation of light and the raising of consciousness. It has a quality of beauty and the realization that the light of beauty shines within and radiates without. In *'Tantra of Sound'*, Jonathan Goldman states *"the Angel chakra's midway location between the third eye and crown suggests that it possesses qualities that are a little more spiritual than the third eye, and a little less transpersonal than the crown chakra."*

Crown (Sahasrara) Note B

Physical level – This chakra is traditionally where all of the energies of the other chakras are realized. It is connected with the top of the skull, the pineal, hair, skin and the central nervous system. The pineal gland is responsible for the production of melatonin and regulates our internal body clock. Melatonin is also thought to have anti-aging properties and is believed to affect the pituitary, thyroid, adrenals and gonads, which could account for the physical connectedness of this chakra to the others. The pineal is the control center for the effective functioning of our physical, mental and emotional selves.

Emotional level – Emotions that are associated with separation from the self and the source could resonate in this chakra as can emotions around being able to trust the divine process of life. This chakra can also be connected to anxiety that may result due to feeling disassociated from the mind of God. If a person is emotionally ungrounded and feels disconnected this could result in anxiety disorders such as panic attacks.

Mental level – This chakra is related to thought and understanding. It is connected with thoughts we have around our divine connection and the radiating or withholding of divine spiritual energy from ourselves and others. It is also related to being open minded to spiritual activities and religious practices.

Spiritual level – On the spiritual level this chakra is related to our spiritual identity and our relationship with the universe. It receives, transmutes and transmits the finest divine energy. In the Vedic system this chakra is known as the "thousand petaled lotus". According to some accounts Kundalini energy flowing up the central channel can only reach the crown when all of the other chakras are functioning correctly. If you have a balanced crown chakra you are able to fully experience the connectedness of all things.

The chakras as a developmental model

The chakras can be seen as a developmental or evolutionary model. Although we give and receive energy through each of our chakras all the time there are times when our life experiences filter through one chakra more then the other. In my opinion, a greater understanding of our relationship with the chakra system and how we relate to our world can be reached if we see our chakras from this point of view.

If you think about the films and books that feature a castaway situation most will follow the same developmental stages. Imagine you are marooned on a desert island with a small group of people that have never met each other before. The first thing you would do is to make sure your physical needs were met. It is unlikely that you would crawl onto dry land and immediately begin building a shrine to your God or Goddess (although you may thank them for your survival!). The first thing you would probably do is check for injuries and deal with those first. Then you'd probably explore the island, looking for a source of food and fresh water. You would then build your shelter in a safe place close to the food and water. All of these needs relate to the base chakra.

When you knew you had your basic needs met you might then look at forming relationships. Most groups or tribes want to get on at first and so it is unlikely that in the first stages of being marooned there would be any fighting unless your physical survival was threatened. Relationships will then begin to form, including those of a sexual nature. At this stage there is a certain amount of give and take within the group until a hierarchy is established. This stage of group development is related to the sacral chakra.

When the group hierarchy starts forming there will be people who want to lead and control as well as those who are happy to be led. As control mechanisms and rules begin to evolve within the group there will be those that feel secure and those that feel threatened and resist. This is where the group is testing its strength and cohesion and this process is related to the solar plexus chakra. Fighting can begin which will either be resolved or result in the group splintering into other groups. This is the pivotal point; the "love and power point".

If a group is able to transcend the power struggles they can reach a place of mutual acceptance and unconditional love. Even resistance is met with love and support. The group encourages transparency and honesty and openly explores the resistance objectively and without attachment to outcomes. This open and honest communication is where the heart, thymus and throat chakras work together.

Once communication is flowing the group is able to think about where they are going as an entity. There will be people who see their future path being off the island and they may make plans to build rafts and make the journey back home. There may be others in the group who would like to stay and therefore their vision for the future will be different. This is related to the zeal point and brow chakra.

Once they have settled into their vision and feel comfortable with where they are the group that has chosen to stay may begin to consider "higher" energies such as communicating with the divine realms. Spiritual beliefs and practices may come into the frame. This is connected to the angel and crown chakras.

During each stage of development the group may be challenged and entrained as control mechanisms and survival issues come into play which can pull the energy into the base, sacral and solar plexus chakras. If the group are able to filter their experiences through all of the chakras in a healthy and balanced way and transcend its "stuff" individually and collectively they could create paradise on Earth.

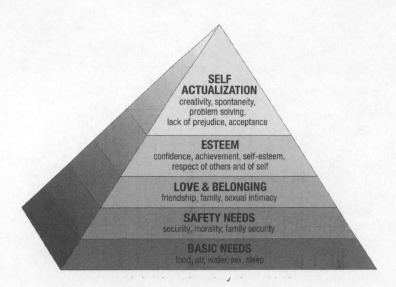

In 1954 Abraham Maslow introduced a developmental model which he called "the hierarchy of needs". Maslow was a psychologist who developed a framework of human potential which follows the natural development of the chakra system very well. He categorized the various levels of need which drive a human being and felt that when a lower and more pressing need was satisfied a person feels their motivation shift to a new need at a higher level until the ultimate state of self-actualization is reached.

Exercise: Feeling the chakras

Aim: The aim of this exercise is to get to know your chakras and to improve communication between you, your chakras and your environment.

You may find it easier to do this exercise every night before you go to sleep and every morning when you first wake up as you will already be in a relaxed state, but choose the time that suits you best. Once you get used to the way you communicate with your chakras, you'll find you will receive information whilst you are at work, in the bath or even shopping! Having said that, do put time aside to scan your chakras as you can gain so much more from your sessions by working in a clear and focused way.

Moving from base to crown spend time tuning in to each of the chakras in turn, noting how each one feels. What shape is it? Does it have a color, memory, feeling, emotion, physical sensation, image or anything else associated with it? Do you get the sense that the chakra is sluggish or overactive? Spend several minutes on each chakra and write down your findings, however strange they may seem. One of my students once saw their base chakra as a blue boot which may sound bizarre to us but they knew exactly what it meant to them.

If you are unable to interpret your findings don't worry, it really doesn't matter. Don't try to force a reason why you have experienced a chakra in a certain way, let it go, you may find the answer tumbles into your mind in a day or so.

The chakras and the musical scale

Many sound therapists and practitioners have a system of notes, sounds and/or vowels which they attribute to different chakras. If you look back at the chakra correspondences you will see that I have placed the note that I use next to the description of each chakra. Often I am asked the question *"why do you use a different note for each chakra?"*

There are a few answers to this question. On a very practical level if you were to go to a sound practitioner and they were to play the same bowl for almost an hour every time you saw them this would not be very interesting and would only be exposing your system to a certain frequency (unless there was a particular reason for them to do this). In the BAST method of sound therapy practitioners create a sonic prescription that is unique to each individual depending on their imbalances. We also use intervals created by different tones to create different energetic effects. There are other sound practitioners and therapists who also work in this way but if you are working for self-healing you may not want to have a full chakra set of crystal and/or Himalayan bowls.

In this instance, one of the keys to working with sound for self-healing and transformation is intention.

If you want to use a crystal bowl tuned to C to work solely on your base chakra, then it *is* your base chakra bowl. We also know that intention does not just operate at an individual level but also a collective level. The more people that use the same system, the greater the collective energy source will be. By using a system (and this includes any system) all we are doing at an energetic level is aligning to the belief that a certain note is used for a certain chakra. This raises another question *"do I have to believe it is going to work?"* My answer to this is *"no"*, not consciously anyway. Many people I have worked with have been skeptical about the effectiveness of sound and yet still experienced a recovery from their symptoms. Alignment to the belief may reinforce the wholing process but it is not essential as the entraining energy of the collective will help as well as the intention of the practitioner.

In the East certain words have been used to resonate with the chakras for thousands of years. The sacred seed syllables, or "Bija" are potentially no more or less effective than notes of the musical scale. It is down to the intention of the practitioner, the intention of the receiver and the alignment to the collective energy source. The more you work with any system the more resonance this system will have for you. Many sound practitioners in the West use the western musical scale because the notes are already programmed into the Western person's antenna array. This means that there is potentially less resistance to the system accepting these frequencies as they are not "alien" to our ears. At the end of the day any note is just a frequency which we give a name so that we can identify it and organize it in a musical context.

The Nadis

The idea that we have energy channels as well as chakras first appeared in the Upanishads almost three thousand years ago.

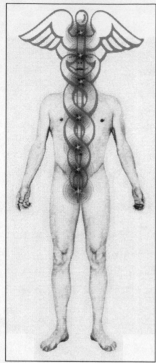

The Nadis

The nadis are energy channels that are similar to meridians in the traditional system of Chinese medicine. These energy channels convey prana throughout the system, just as the meridians covey chi. There are many different accounts as to how many nadis actually exist (some say there are thousands) but in this book we will be concentrating on three; the pingala, ida and sushumna nadis.

The ida and pingala nadis are a manifestation of the masculine and feminine energies within us. This has nothing to do with gender as energy is gender neutral, but it is more to do with the quality of the energy. If you prefer you can use the terms "active" and "receptive" instead. They start at the base chakra and terminate at the brow crossing between each chakra as they move up the body. Some say that where the ida and pingala cross a whirlpool of energy is formed which creates the chakra.

The pingala nadi, meaning *"sun channel"* or *"tawny current"* in Sanskrit is the active energy channel and is orange-red in color. It starts on the right side of the base chakra, twisting and turning in a serpentine manner between the chakras and terminating at the brow chakra. The ida nadi or *"soothing current"* is the lunar current. It is receptive, white like the moon and starts at the left side of the base chakra. The left side of the body has long been associated with being more receptive in energy and the right side more active and this could be one of the reasons why.

The sushumna is the *"divine current"* and is rather like an energetic spinal column. Just as our spine supports our body the sushumna is a central channel which supports the chakras. The sushumna is a conduit between the universal source and the earth. In his book *"Chakras and Nadis"* Swami Atmananda states *"it has aspects such as faith in divinity, nourishment and revelation and is the channel through which evolution takes place. Kundalini energy rises through the sushumna connecting the person to the divine source"*.

Imbalance in the nadis can manifest in an imbalance of the active and receptive energetic principles within. If you feel that these principles are imbalanced you can tailor make a sounding session to suit your needs. The sound sessions will help to achieve a balance in a general sense and the rhythm exercises have certain applications when balancing the active and receptive principles. By balancing the nadis as well as the chakras the energy centers are nourished and the energy source available to you is infinite.

Listening to the nadis

In my experience the nadis can give us a wealth of information on our health and wellbeing. When I have been doing a lot of mental work, such as writing or preparing lessons, the sound of my nadis is louder and somewhat like tinnitus. I believe this is due to my mental level being overworked. This sound tells me that I need to balance my system with a sound session. Five minutes or more of "sonic hot chocolate" really helps bring the volume down!

Over the years I have successfully treated many people who have had tinnitus-like symptoms. Tinnitus is caused by damage to the cilia in the cochlea due to loud sounds and certain drugs and neurological conditions can also cause tinnitus-like symptoms. I believe that what many people consider to be tinnitus is actually an imbalance of the nadis due to stress in the system on some level. In these cases more often than not the tinnitus improves after just one session and continues to get better with each session thereafter.

Being able to hear our own energy system is not widely known in the West so it is natural to think that we have tinnitus when we hear ringing in the ears. If you have not been to a loud concert, taken strong medication or had any dizziness or balance problems then it could be that your nadis are talking to you. In some cases tinnitus can point to a serious condition, so if you have sudden onset acute tinnitus for no reason or it is in one ear more than the other it is wise to go to your GP for a check-up.

Exercise: your inner realms
Aim: The aim of this exercise is to get in touch with your nadis.

The more familiar you become with your nadis the more information you will have about your energy system and general state of being. You will be able to tell if your system is overactive and act accordingly by introducing a calming exercise into your wholing sessions. For this exercise you will need a good set of earplugs which you can get from a pharmacist.

Spend twenty minutes tuning in to your inner realms and write down all of the different sounds that you hear. Don't worry too much about the sound of your breath, circulation or digestion (although these can also have messages for you so give them a little attention and then move on). What you are focusing on are the high-pitched whistling or low rumbling sounds that do not belong to your belly!

Really tune into each sound and notice if the sound divides into other sounds. Tune in at the end of every day over a period of a few weeks and see if the different tasks you do change your inner sounds. How do your nadis sound when you have had a busy day compared to a relaxing day? You can also try this exercise before and after a wholing session and see if there is a difference. After a while you will get to know how your energy system is responding to the sound which will add another dimension to your sessions.

"Breath of the Gods and life-cell of the world, He freely wanders. We devote our veneration to Him whose voice we hear but whose form no one sees."

The Rig-Veda

Sacred Listening

To truly listen to yourself and others is a gift. According to Kay Lindahl, author of *"The Sacred Art of Listening"* *"listening is being fully present to spirit to self and to others"*. How many times do you "zone out" of a conversation? All of us flit between listening and non-listening when we are relating to others, and often we don't listen to ourselves fully either. In many spiritual teachings true listening is considered a sacred act, but why?

The cochlea in the inner ear is where sound-waves are transformed into electrical impulses that the brain interprets into the sounds that we hear. It is a spiral of two and a half turns that conforms to the sacred proportion of the golden mean so apart from anything else there is sacred geometry at the center of our hearing mechanism.

Next time you are having a conversation with someone listen to every word they are saying. True listening is listening beyond the words. When you open your ears to everything you begin to hear so much more. After a while you may find that your antenna array becomes more sensitive and your whole body becomes an ear. When this happens your perception grows and you transcend beyond the word to the intention behind the words. This extra sensory perception yields so many rewards as you are able to *feel* a conversation as well as hear it. This is sacred listening.

Exercise: Sacred listening

Aim: The aim of this exercise is to train yourself to listen in a sacred way.

The next time you have a conversation with a friend or family member, practice sacred listening. Give that person as much undivided attention as you can. Notice what happens when you *choose* to listen. How long are you able to focus on the person who is speaking before drifting off? What causes you to drift off? Is it when a certain subject is spoken about? If so, does the subject have a resonance for you? When you are speaking to another person can you tell when they are fully listening to you and when they zone out? When someone gives you their full and undivided attention notice how this feels and thank them for listening fully.

*Silence. It is alive. A drop of silence. My ears penetrate it. I am inside
it. The drop becomes a universe, a cosmos that begins to resound.*
Johachim – Ernst Berendt

The Sound of Silence

Imagine that you are walking in the woods at night and come
across an old deserted house. You walk up to the door and reach
around for the light but the electricity was switched off long ago.
You turn on your flashlight and go into the house. As you step
through the front door the flashlight suddenly goes out and you
hear a rustle somewhere inside the house. You freeze, holding your
breath, daring not to make a sound. Your senses stretch out as far
as they can go in order to pick up the slightest sound or movement.

Your natural reaction in the above scenario was to become
absolutely still and quiet. In order for you to *really* hear, you first
need to become silent. This was my experience when I became ill
with ME. I was confined to my bed and it was only when I stopped
and surrendered to the process that I was able to hear my system
talking to me. It was not long before I knew exactly what to do to
transcend the holding patterns that I had created for myself.

How can we fully appreciate sound unless we have experienced the sacredness of silence? At the beginning of every sound
session I leave a few moments to acknowledge the silence from
which everything came; the point before the big bang; the bindu;
the void. Then I begin to play softly, gently allowing the sound
to come from the silence. At the end of a sound session I allow
the sound to gently subside and let the silence take over once
again enveloping the levels of my being. It is in this silence that
I often feel the effects of the sound in my body the most. In
silence you can hear the mind of God resonating within and
without. According to Jill Purce, *"being able to listen is essential...in
this way you complete a circuit of attention that enables you to go
beyond the thinking mind"*.

Silence is a gift and one that needs to be given time and space.

Have a look at your life and assess how much silence you embrace. One could argue that absolute silence is not possible, and after experiencing the sound of your nadis you will know that even in the most silent places your body is humming. But it is necessary to embrace silence, stillness and quietude in your life for you to be able to align to the mind of God. Think about what silence means to you and reflect on whether you feel there is enough silence in your life to achieve a balance. How much silence do you feel you need to balance your energy system?

Do you need to have the television or radio on all the time for "background noise"? When I suggest the concept of embracing silence to people they sometimes say *"I need to have some sound all of the time"* or *"the first thing I do when I wake up is switch on the television for some background noise"*. Statements like this can point to an imbalance. When I ask about the need for constant sound they say things like *"I need to feel there is someone else in the house"* or *"I use it as a distraction"*. I find these explanations fascinating as they can point to a wealth of different underlying core messages and imbalances.

When I was a child I used to get the giggles in quiet places such as libraries or examinations. I felt the need to make sound as *"quiet places made me nervous"*. Since then I have worked through the issues of anxiety that manifested in the form of giggles and I now *love* the silence, it is my friend. To enable us to align to the mind of God and receive guidance for our personal transformation we need silence.

Noise can affect the communication process. We all know how it feels to try to communicate with someone when there is a loud or distracting noise going on but noise doesn't have to be audible. If you are in a classroom being taught by the most gorgeous person, are you listening to every word they are saying or are you distracted by the color of their eyes or their smile? This type of distraction is known as "semantic noise". Be aware of the semantic noise in your life. What distracts you from embracing silence? Make a note of what comes up when you ask yourself this question and subject the answers to a loving enquiry, you may be amazed at what comes up!

Exercise: Silence is golden

Aim: The aim of this exercise is to allow silence into your life as well as becoming aware of any inner resonances that sounds in your everyday life can create.

You'll need to put aside at least twenty minutes without distractions for this exercise. Sit down and close your eyes for a few moments to tune yourself in. This closes down the visual antenna array. After a while begin to make notes of all of the sounds you hear. You will need to open your eyes to write, but then close them again and tune back in or if you prefer you can use a voice recorder so that you are not distracted by the writing process or you can write the whole session up at the end if you are happy to remember everything that came up for you. Look for resonances within the chakras and/or levels of being as you interact with your outer realms. Are any core messages or beliefs being triggered? Here is an example.

"I was sitting in my garden on a Sunday afternoon and I became aware of the sound of children playing in a neighboring garden. Their laughter came in waves on the breeze. As I tuned in to their sound I felt my heart chakra expand and I was reminded of how it felt to be carefree and young. I felt a lovely warm feeling wash over me as my heart centre expanded followed by sadness as I feel that I won't ever be able to experience that wonderful joy of childhood again. I was then reminded of a girl that used to bully me and my solar plexus tightened up. She made me feel so scared, the cow! I had a lump in my throat and felt my energy sink. I wish I'd had the courage to tell her how I felt but I am such a coward. Suddenly a plane flew over and my attention was taken to all of those people sitting in the sky above me. I wondered where they were going and I remembered my last holiday in Marrakech with pleasure. I could smell the spices wafting through the markets and immediately felt relaxed as I remembered the lovely massage I had there. My solar plexus relaxed and I was once again enveloped in a warm feeling"

You can see that there is a lot of opportunity to explore what has come up in this short example. Be as open and honest as you can. At the end of the exercise enjoy the sound of the world around you without writing for a few moments before finishing.

It is ideal to do this exercise in different places at different times of the day as you will find that sound carries differently depending on the temperature of the air. The animals who inhabit our world by day sound different to the creatures of the night. The sound of the rush hour traffic may create different resonances than the sounds of the "thump thump" of music coming from bars in the evening, but investigate the resonances found during each session before moving to the next so that you can fully process each level of this exercise and listen to the messages that the silence has for you.

Even when you are not consciously listening your ears are always on alert. When you sleep the sound-waves in the air are moving the eardrum which translates down the tiny bones in the inner ear into cochlea, the sacred temple of the inner ear. A part of your brain is decoding the sounds and deciding if they are a threat to your safety. This is one of the reasons why we often find it hard to sleep in a new place for the first night or two as the brain will wake you when it registers a new or unfamiliar sound. Once these sounds have been programmed into the system and the brain has learned that they are no threat to you the body will be allowed to sleep through the night.

When you are not in a listening session your system will still be resonating with the sounds you are hearing so the more attuned you become the more messages you will be getting, which means the more opportunities for you to become enlightened.

"All that one sees, smells, feels, tastes, and hears is through the channel of the breath."
Hazrat Inayat Khan

The Breath of Life

From your first inhalation to your final exhalation your breath sustains you through your life. Breathing is an art-form and an excellent tool for self-diagnosis. Most of us breathe perfectly naturally when we are born but then begin to loose the art of correct breathing as we get older due to holding patterns and the way we interact with our environment. By examining the pattern of your breath you will be able to determine how you react to your environment which will give you vital clues to the imbalances in your system. Donna Farhi, author of *"The Breathing Book"* writes, *"When your breathing becomes unconsciously altered the autonomic part of your nervous system resets itself so that breathing becomes automatically disordered and automatically restricted"*. This relates to the unhealthy patterns that we can adopt due to an underlying core message that has become dense enough to alter our breathing patterns. Farhi believes that somewhere between the unconscious breath and consciously directed breath lies the essential breath. She writes, *"essential breath, a conscious flow that arises out of a background that is still and silent and dissolves back into this same stillness."* By reprogramming these underlying patterns you can recover your true essence, your *"essential breath"*. It is interesting to note that she also mentions the importance of stillness which we know is vital to aligning to the mind of God.

By practicing the various breathing techniques in this section you will increase the flow of prana in your system, tone up the lungs and diaphragms and massage your internal organs. As a result you may well notice an improvement in your overall health and well-being. As well as this your voice may become more supported and you may be able to hold notes for longer when conducting vocal sounding sessions. As the sound can be carried inward on the breath as well as outward on the voice, there is a wonderful relationship that the breath has with sound. You may experience a whole new dimension when combining your breathing techniques with your sound-work.

Breathing is an interaction between you and the universal energy source. When you are exhaling you are giving to the universe and when you inhale you are receiving from the universe. As everything is energy, as well as taking in oxygen, you are also taking in prana when you breathe. The breath alone is a powerful diagnostic tool as well as a vehicle for profound transformation. The breath moves us, creating a wave that ebbs and flows throughout the physical body. It has the power to lower or quicken the heart rate and respiration and can control the extreme pain of labor. The breath calms the mental body by slowing the brainwaves and soothes and stabilizes the emotional body during anxiety or stress. The spiritual body also expands on the breath taking us to new levels of consciousness.

On a physical level breathing is basically the constriction and release of the lungs. Imagine you are holding a dry sponge in your hand. If you were to squeeze the sponge in your fist until all of the air had gone this is like the lungs on a full exhale with the diaphragm squeezing out all of the air. If you release the sponge from your grip it will automatically spring back and fill with air. This is exactly what your lungs will do when they are allowed to but tension in the diaphragms can prevent this wonderful relaxed and effortless breath from occurring. We use the words "take a breath" when we ask people to breathe in or relax, but this conveys a subconscious message which implies that there is effort in breathing, that we actually "take" our breath (if you were to take an apple from a pile you would reach out and grasp it). If we compare the constriction and release of the breath to the constriction and release of our energy system we can easily see that an imbalance in the breath may also translate to other areas of the system. When we allow ourselves to breathe without constriction our body breathes us; we do not need to take air in at all.

According to Hazrat Inayat Khan in a paper written specifically on "pasi anfas" (breath work), *the whole mechanism of the body works by the power of the breath and every disorder in the working of the mechanism is caused by some irregularity in the breath*". Breathing techniques have been adopted by spiritual practitioners for thousands of years. There has been much research that demonstrates that our breath has an impact on our brainwaves and also the chemicals that are released in the body. Peptides are an important part of our body chemistry as they play a role in regulating almost all biological processes. In *"Molecules of Emotion"*, Candice Pert writes, *"If the cell is the engine that drives all life, then the receptors are the buttons on the control panel of that engine, and a specific peptide (or other kind of ligand) is the finger that pushes the button and gets things started"*. Different breath patterns can influence the type and amount of peptides that are released from the brain stem. According to Pert, *"virtually any peptide found anywhere else can be found in the respiratory center. This peptide substrate may provide the scientific rationale for the powerful healing effects of consciously controlled breath patterns"*.

Your breath is a mirror of your inner thoughts and feelings. If you have a sudden shock it is very likely that you will take a quick, sharp gasp of air and then hold it momentarily. If you are stressed your breathing may become shallow and you may even hold your breath. Breathing directly influences the chemicals that are released from the brain stem as well as the amount of prana in your system.

Exercise: Breath awareness

Aim: The aim of this exercise is to develop breath awareness.

Keep a record of your breathing patterns throughout a

normal week. Tune in to your breathing during different activities in your day and notice where you breathe from. Are there times when you are breathing from the upper part of the lungs and times when you are breathing from the lower part of the lungs? Use your normal resting breath as a base line (you can monitor this when you are just about to go to sleep at night). Examine your breath when you first wake up and also at different times of the day and write down what you find. Are there times when you hold your breath, such as when you see something on television or during a particular daily activity? Do your shoulders hunch towards your ears when you breathe? Keep a breath journal for a week look back to see if there are any patterns and investigate what you find.

Upper chest breathing

There is evidence to show that people who breathe from the upper chest are more likely to develop neck, upper back and shoulder tension, headaches, eye tension and even heart disease. People who are feeling the stresses and strains of modern day living tend to breathe from the upper part of the lungs, taking in shallow and fast gasps of air. The action of shallow breathing is useful for sprinters who tend to use the upper parts of the lungs when they are running a race, but not so good for everyday life!

Exercise: Upper and lower chest breathing

Aim: The aim of this exercise is to feel what it is like to breathe from different parts of the lungs.

Stand in a relaxed posture position with feet slightly apart. Place one hand on the upper part of the chest over the thymus chakra and another on the solar plexus. Aim to breathe only into the upper part of the chest. The upper hand should move up and down and the lower hand should be still. Do this for a few moments. How do you feel? Most people use words such as *"anxious"*, *"restricted"* and *"constricted"* to describe the feeling of this breath.

When I have worked with asthma sufferers they have told me that this breath feels similar in energy to that of an asthma attack and one person actually felt that she may trigger an attack if she continued to breathe in this way. Physically your shoulders, upper back and chest may tighten and your shoulders may rise up towards your ears. The upper body tends to feel "stuck". A few moments of breathing from the upper chest restricts the energy flow to the rest of the body and changes the body chemistry.

Now move your breath to the hand that is on your belly. Isolate the upper chest so that it remains still and fill up the bottom of the lungs but not the top. People often use the words *"relaxing" "centering"* and *"calming"* to describe the effects of this type of breathing.

Now move to the complete breath. Keep one hand on your upper chest and one on your belly. Inhaling through the nose slowly and steadily breathe into the base of your lungs as if you were filling up a balloon from the bottom up. When the base of your lungs are full continue to breathe slowly, filling the top of the lungs. Notice if there is any tension or restriction anywhere and avoid hunching the shoulders. Your hands should move in a wave-like motion, with the hand that is on your belly being slowly followed by the hand on your chest. Then exhale steadily through the mouth. The complete breath exercise is beneficial when you need to calm your system and release tension from the upper chest, back, neck and shoulders.

Diaphragmatic breathing

The lungs have no musculature therefore they are not capable of breathing by themselves. The solar plexus diaphragm enables breathing to take place by acting as the powerhouse that squeezes the air out of the lungs on the exhale. If the lungs and diaphragm are allowed to do their job properly the inhale happens of its own accord. Just as the air floods back into the sponge when the grip is released, the air will flow back into the lungs easily when the diaphragm is released.

If we look back at the line of constriction and release, most symptoms that have constrictive patterns involve holding of some kind. This could translate to your breathing, causing the diaphragm to become held in some way. If you have problems letting go of the diaphragm does this translate to other areas of your life? Are you trying to control any aspect of your life? Do you have problems letting go of things? As the diaphragm is situated in the solar plexus you may find that an imbalance in this chakra could translate to the diaphragm and therefore inhibit your breathing.

Exercise: The sponge

Aim: The aim of this exercise is to illustrate that the inhale happens of its own accord. It also removes the stale air from the lungs and tones them up, releasing oxygen and prana into the system. It is also a very useful exercise to build muscle memory in the diaphragm, re-programming it to be able to release and let go.

Stand with the legs shoulder width apart and your hands on your hips. Imagine you have a huge cake in front of you with hundreds of candles on it. Take a big breath in and exhale as if you were blowing out all the candles in one long sustained blow. Don't force your breath out too quickly or strain anything in the process! Squeeze every last bit of your breath out of the lungs then take a tiny gasp of breath in and blow out even further. You may well find that you have more air to blow out than you breathed in. After you have squeezed the lungs like a sponge all you need to do is let go in the diaphragm area and the air will flow back into the lungs in an easy and gentle way. Repeat this exercise three times. If you feel too dizzy or uncomfortable at any time stop or do the exercise sitting down. The dizziness is the flood of oxygen entering your bloodstream. If you have been breathing incorrectly for a long time the dizziness will be more apparent so you can use this exercise as an indication of how you have been breathing in the past.

If you feel you are holding your diaphragm then you can try the following exercise which helps to loosen everything up.

Exercise: The diaphragm bounce

Aim: The aim of this exercise is to loosen and tone the diaphragm.

Stand with your legs shoulder width apart and let go of any tension in the diaphragm and belly area. Keep your feet on the floor and bend your knees to bounce your body in short, fairly quick bounces (not too fast!). Relax the belly and you will feel the weight of the diaphragm pulling little gasps of air into the lungs. If your diaphragm is relaxed you will find that you don't need to take a breath and that the energy of your bounce is breathing you. You can take this exercise a stage further and introduce a "Ha, Ha, Ha" sound as you bounce. With practice you will be able to chant American Indian style without taking a breath. If you feel too dizzy at any time, stop.

Every time you notice tension in the diaphragm let it go. At first it may seem as though you are doing this a lot, but if you persevere you will re-program your body and tension or holding in the diaphragm will disappear.

The diaphragms

We have three diaphragms that are involved when we take a full breath. They are situated at the base of the lungs, the pelvic floor and in the throat. All of the diaphragms are related to each other and therefore constriction in one will have an influence on the function of the others. As you breathe in each of the diaphragms move to make space for the breath to come into the body.

The solar plexus diaphragm is a dome-shaped muscle situated at the base of the lungs dividing the chest from the stomach. As

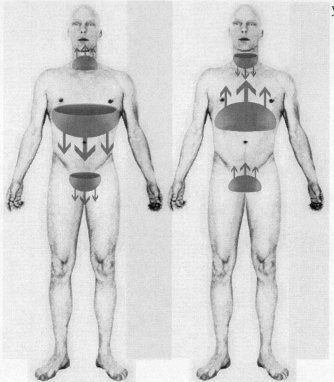

The three diaphragms on inhalation.   *The three diaphragms on exhalation.*

The Three Diaphragms

breathe in the lungs and ribs expand, the diaphragm is flattened and pushed down and the abdominal muscles are pressed down and out. The direction of movement of the solar plexus diaphragm is outwards and downwards when you inhale and inwards and upwards when you exhale. It is common for there to be tension in the solar plexus diaphragm, especially in the West. Many women are sensitive about their bellies as they are confronted by flat stomachs every time they turn on the television or open a magazine. In recent years an increasing number of men are working to have a stomach that you could grate cheese on! Holding in the stomach is unnatural and can cause tension in the diaphragms as well as the rest of the body. The pelvic diaphragm is actually two diaphragms which broaden and move downwards when you inhale. Tension in the pelvic diaphragm can indicate an imbalance in the sacral chakra and can lead to inflexibility in the hip area and lower back pain. The vocal diaphragm is also dome shaped and is situated in the larynx between the throat and the base of the tongue. When you inhale it moves upwards and outwards and inwards and downwards when you exhale. Tension in the vocal diaphragm can translate to the throat chakra and cause tension in the neck and shoulders.

Constriction in any of the diaphragms also has a direct impact on the voice. If the lungs are not able to expand you will need to take more breaths than someone who is flexible and your voice could sound weak and unsupported. All of the diaphragms should be toned rather than flabby as they support the voice, but they also need to be flexible and able to expand to allow air fully into the lungs.

When doing the complete breath exercise send your awareness to the three diaphragms when you inhale, directing the breath into the base of the lungs. Release the sacral diaphragm, feeling the expansion in the pelvis and across the lower back and hips. Release the solar plexus diaphragm as you continue to fill up the lungs and send your attention to the vocal diaphragm, feeling the release in the upper back, neck, chest, throat and shoulders. Release and allow the air to flood back in naturally. Repeat this several times.

Exercise: The purification breath

Aim: This exercise was given by Hazrat Inayat Khan to his mureeds (students) as a basic practice to prepare for meditation and healing work. This exercise can be used to prepare for a sounding session. It uses the elements, colors and visualization. You will need to count as you breathe. The aim is to allow more time for the exhale until the body naturally draws the breath in.

Earth

Visualize the color yellow and imagine your energy spreading out

Breathe in through the nose to the count of four

Hold for the count of one

Breathe out to the count of six

Water

Visualize the color turquoise and imagine your energy flowing downwards

Breathe in through the nose to the count of four

Hold for the count of one

Breathe out for the count of eight

Fire

Visualize the color golden-red and imagine your energy moving upwards

Breathe in through the mouth to the count of four

Hold for the count of one

Breathe out for the count of ten

Air

Visualize the color transparent blue and imagine your energy dispersing

Breathe in through the mouth to the count of four

Hold for the count of one

Breathe out through the nose to the count of fourteen

To ground yourself after this exercise you can return to the earth-breath.

As you can see from this exercise it is encouraging the release of the breath. You can use this exercise when you feel your system is moving towards the constriction side of the scale.

Part 2 Sounding the Mind of God

*"The knower of the mystery of sound knows the mystery of
the whole universe."*
Hazrat Inayat Kahn

Introduction

The second half of this book concentrates on the use of sound as
a powerful tool for self-healing and transformation. In this
section we will be examining different instruments and
techniques and putting them together to create wonderful
sounding sessions designed specifically to suit your needs.
Please make sure that you are fully grounded after doing any of
the exercises in this section (see the chapter on grounding if you
require further information).

When I began working with sound I found that each
instrument moved my system in a different way. I spent many
years communicating with the energy of different instruments,
and as each one told me its story I was able to see how I could
apply this to helping to improve health and wellbeing. This
wonderful journey continues as I discover new instruments. I
also find that the longer I work with an instrument, the more it
reveals to me. It is as if new chapters of the story unfold as the
years progress. If you are planning to use a variety of instruments take time to get to know each one and integrate each
exercise before moving on to the next. In the West we can often
be seduced by the "I want it all and I want it now" culture. If you
allow yourself and each instrument time and space your
relationship will deepen, offering greater potential for personal
growth and development. These experiences are blissful and
carry many messages that are life-affirming and energy
expanding. Enjoy!

An understanding of the waveform means to understand that all
things change, that nothing is static.
Jonathan Goldman

Wave Patterns and the Particles of Love and Hate

You are the sum-total of everything you have ever experienced in your life (and lives) so far. The use of different instruments can allow you to reach a new level of being. It is rather like exercise. If you spend all of your time swimming you may find that after an hour in a spinning class you had aches in pains in muscles you never thought you had! This is because the muscle groups that you use for swimming are different than those you use for cycling. It is very similar with different instruments. Using another instrument can help you identify new resonances in your system.

Depending on your imbalance you may prefer to work with one instrument rather than another or you may prefer to work gradually through a series of different instruments, gently transmuting the energy held at different levels. A little knowledge of the sound and energy signatures of the different instruments we will be working with could help you to choose which instrument could help with certain imbalances.

Remember Dr. Fred Alan Wolf's "hate" and "love" particles? We know that particles in smaller boxes (belief systems, patterns, symptoms) are more resistant to change and when they do the change can be more drastic and unstable. We also know that particles in a large box remain flexible, making small and continuous changes. Through the laws of sympathetic resonance and entrainment the sound will penetrate the body at a cellular level, resonating with certain areas of your being and allowing denser energy to become more flexible.

By examining the energy signature (sound-wave pattern) of different instruments we are able to get a good idea of which instruments could help certain symptoms. For example, the sound-wave pattern of a Himalayan bowl is more erratic than that of a crystal bowl due to the amount of harmonics contained in a Himalayan bowl. The Himalayan bowl is rich and warm and their harmonics are energy expanding. I find the Himalayan bowls really beneficial if you are beginning a session as they give you a wonderfully warm sonic cuddle and allow your energy field to gently begin to expand. If you are new to sound work a Himalayan bowl is a really good place to begin sounding the mind of God.

The sound signature of a crystal bowl is open and expanded. In my experience the crystal bowls are very good for expanding holding patterns further and reaching another level of being in a gentle yet powerful way. The sound-wave of a crystal bowl is very similar in nature to the energy in a large box. It is smoother and less erratic. I believe that it is the similarity between these two sound-wave signatures that enables sympathetic resonance to take place, allowing for greater expansion of your energy field. Sometimes with denser, tighter energy patterns there can be too much of a mis-match between the energy signature of the pattern and that of the sound, which is why I tend to prefer to start working on denser patterns with instruments that have a slightly more erratic sound signature, such as the Himalayan bowls, voice or drum.

The voice also has a more erratic wave form but as we produce this from within it has a quality that no other instrument has. According to Hazrat Inayat Khan, *"when one compares the voice with the instrument, there is no real comparison, because the voice is life itself"*. The voice contacts our innermost realms and communicates our feelings, secrets, suffering and desires to the outer realms through the vehicle of the breath. The voice is a perfect tool for expressing and externalizing held energy.

The drum also has an erratic wave pattern. Rhythm is the root of tone and the drum was one of the first instruments to be used by man and womankind. Perhaps this is why the drum touches us on such a deep level. When a drum is struck you hear tones and harmonics which blend together as the tempo increases. Regular rhythm also entrains our brainwaves. The drum is one of the most physical of the instruments we will be working with in this book as not only does it require a certain amount of stamina (especially during a drum journey) but you can feel the sound-waves massaging your body, gently buffeting denser energy patterns, coaxing them to become more flexible and expansive.

Some people will resonate with one instrument more than another which is perfectly natural but an obvious emotional aversion to an instrument indicates a resonance within the system. I once treated a client who at the end of a treatment where I had used different instruments including the crystal bowls, said *"I really didn't like those awful crystal bowls, they made me want to run out of the room!"* I asked him to identify the emotion he was feeling and he said it was fear. The crystal bowls had resonated with fear held within his system and had triggered a fight or flight response. This gave me a really good indication as to how to conduct future sessions to gently transmute the fear. As a result this person was able to completely clear their irritable bowel syndrome and the problems he had been experiencing in his personal life were also resolved and he now loves the crystal bowls!

If you feel aversion to working with a particular instrument then you may find it useful to reflect on whether this is resonating with anything held within you. You may find that once you have transmuted the energy imbalance the aversion to the instrument dissolves.

"The human voice needs no training it is already there, finished and perfect as an entity sounding in the ideal world. What it is waiting for is liberation!"
Valborg Werbeck-Svardstrom

Your Sacred Voice

Your voice is your own personal instrument and your vocal fingerprint. It is coded with everything you have experienced in your life so far, as well as your intention, hopes and dreams. It is a window to your soul and a very powerful way for you to work on imbalances on all levels of being. Your voice can help you expand your energy, achieve a deep level of relaxation and give you a boost when you are low in energy. According to Jill Purce, *"the voice is the key to spiritual transformation"*. She goes on to say *"through working with the voice we can learn to enter the state known by the Tibetans as 'rigpa', the awareness which combines emptiness with clarity. This leads ultimately to illumination."*

Not everyone's experience with their voice has been a good one. I remember the stress of auditioning for the school choir and I was only 7 years old! I have worked with many people who now have issues around using their voices due to negatively charged experiences at school or in the home where they were told that *"children should be seen and not heard"* by their parents, for example. I have also worked with people who have had negative experiences with regard to their voices in their adult lives. As we covered in Part 1, these experiences can easily be turned into core messages which then go on to form patterns of resistance in the system. Working through some of these resistances can allow your voice to become enriched; your vocal range may broaden allowing the true beauty of your voice to shine through. If you are interested to hear how your voice changes as you transmute your holding patterns you can always record your vocal sessions and play them back in the future. You may be surprised as to how much your voice has transformed!

Research undertaken in the USA has shown that twenty minutes of voice work increases the amount of immunoglobulin A in the saliva so apart from any of the other benefits that working with the voice can give you, twenty minutes of voice work boosts the immune system.

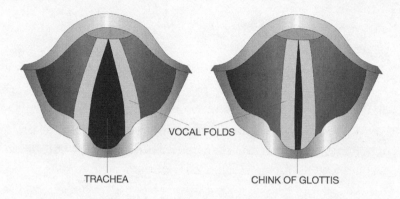

The Vocal Folds

The vocal mechanism

The vocal folds (or vocal cords) are set in the larynx. If you were to stand on the back of your tongue and look down your throat you would see two small folds of skin attached on either side of the windpipe. During breathing they allow the air to pass in and out and when you sing they come together leaving a small opening between them known as the "chink of glottis". As the diaphragm is squeezed the pressure of the air being released from the lungs causes the vocal folds to vibrate. The resonating chambers in the mouth and throat color the sound, adding richness and harmonics and the mouth and tongue shape the sound into vowels and consonants.

Your vocal folds work incredibly hard. For you to sing concert pitch A, which is 440hz, your vocal folds need to vibrate at 440 times *per second!* This is much harder for your voice to do if there is tension or conflict in the vocal folds. The vocal folds have muscles attached to them which move them back and forth at great speed. When you sing a high note your vocal folds stretch long and thin and when you sing a low note they become shorter and flatter.

The vocal folds need flexibility and freedom to enable you to sing a range of notes. Sometimes we get in the way because we are trying to make the vocal mechanism do something outside its natural way of being. Often I see people's heads tip toward the ceiling and almost stand on tiptoes to reach the high notes as if they were stretching to reach something on a very high shelf. This is what we "think" we need to do to "make" the voice reach the notes, but the truth is the vocal mechanism needs to be free to do its own thing. The vocal folds need the opposite of tension to reach the high notes. If we can get out of the way when we are singing the vocal folds can be allowed to produce a wonderfully free and expressive voice and a greater range of sounds. Thinking that our vocal folds "need" to be a certain way causes the mind and vocal mechanism to go into conflict. With the muscles in the vocal mechanism not being allowed to move naturally the mind tries to override the natural process resulting in cracks and breaks in the voice known as *"register breaks"*.

The voice can also be a very useful diagnostic tool. We know that energy in a small box makes erratic changes in state and so when the mind and body are wrestling with each other this can result in the voice leaping unnaturally from one note to another. In some people this can be more apparent in their speaking voice rather than their singing voice, but still indicates an imbalance.

The physical level and the voice
It is important that tension on the physical level is released as this has a direct impact on the voice as well as the rest of the system. Try the following exercise.

Exercise: The physical body and the voice
Aim: The aim of this exercise is to feel how tension in the

physical body affects the voice.

Stand for a moment and scream without actually making a sound. Really give it both barrels and notice how your body is affected. You may have found that your thighs, arms, hands, stomach, buttocks, larynx, throat and mouth tightened up when you screamed. You may also have noticed tension in other areas of the body. If your body is "screaming" with tension on the physical level it is easy to see how this can affect the voice.

The physical body provides support for the voice. The diaphragms need to be relaxed, but strong. This does not mean that there is tension but rather a strength that comes from working out the muscles in these areas so that they are able to support the voice. When we think of relaxation we may think of collapse, just as you may flop onto a sofa at the end of a hard day's work. With regard to therapeutic voice work collapse of the physical body will not help to support and sustain the voice so when you are working through the voice exercises in this book make sure you are sitting upright or standing in a relaxed yet supported way. The breathing exercises should help you to work out the muscles needed to produce a wonderfully supported voice as well as helping to assist with balancing the system as a whole.

Stopping in silence helps us to align with the mind of God. The following postural awareness exercise was introduced to me by Michael Deason-Barrow of *Tonalis*. During the workshop I attended he combined the Alexander Technique with voice-work. This provided me with a very powerful insight as to how even the smallest tension on the physical level can translate to the voice. The following exercise is very useful as it helps to highlight holding patterns on the physical level. When you tune into your patterns you can sometimes get an idea why they are there, but we know that we don't always need to have a story behind an imbalance. The most important thing you can do is identify the pattern and keep releasing it. Over time you will re-program your physical body and as a result transform anything related to the pattern on other levels of being.

Exercise: Postural awareness

Aim: The aim of this exercise is to be aware of patterns in the physical body.

Stand with your legs shoulder-width apart. Imagine that you are supported by a cord going through the crown to a point in the center of the universe and through your tailbone to the center of the Earth. This cord holds you firmly but does not pull you taught, so think "firm support" rather than tension. Bring your attention to your feet. Do you distribute your weight evenly or stand with more weight on the balls or heels of your feet? Reflect on what this means to you. Are you always trying to get somewhere, to the next task in the day or the next project in your life? If so is your weight tipping forward? Or are you favoring your heels and therefore do you hold back in life or want to slow down?

How you stand will directly translate to the other muscles in the body as they will be compensating to keep you balanced. Aim for a 50/50 divide of your weight on the balls and heels of the feet. After you have adjusted your weight distribution move upwards from the feet checking in with the ankles, calves, thighs, buttocks, perineum, anus, diaphragms (pelvic, solar plexus and vocal), stomach, hands, arms, chest, shoulders, back, neck, jaw and head. Notice where there is tension and let it go. Breathe into every joint and vertebrae and as you inhale visualize each joint expanding with breath and light.

During this exercise keep revisiting previous areas of tension that you found. The chances are they will have tightened up again due to programming on the physical level. The quicker they re-tighten, often the denser the pattern. As we have already covered, the physical level is the densest so if you have patterns held here it is a good idea to listen to what they are telling you.

Tune into the tension in the body. Is it close to a particular chakra? Does it have a message for you? If so, what is the message? Listen to what the body has to say and then release the tension and readjust your posture. You will be able to re-program the physical body by repeating this exercise as often as you can. When I was introduced to this technique I experienced a lot of pain in the body as my physical level protested strongly against being re-programmed. I persevered every day for two weeks and felt amazing afterwards! Sometimes my students tell me that although they started off with the best intentions they had to stop doing this exercise because it was too painful for them. If aligning your body is painful this indicates physical patterns that are pulling the body out of balance. If this is your experience with this exercise you may prefer to consult a professional body work practitioner or Alexander Technique practitioner and ask for advice; in my experience perseverance with this exercise yields great rewards.

The emotional level and the voice

The voice conveys the emotions very well. Anyone who has ever heard a singer who is in touch with the emotion of a song cannot fail to be moved by the energy of the emotion that is being carried on the singer's voice though the principles of sympathetic resonance and entrainment. To me this is proof that our intention can be carried on the voice. When you are "choked up" with emotion your voice will reflect this. If there is anger, sadness, happiness, fear or love, this will be directly reflected in the voice and carried to the listener.

The mental level and the voice

People who are under stress tend to talk faster because their mind is racing due to the increased level of adrenaline and other stress hormones and chemicals in the body. The voice can also be higher in pitch due to the tension around the vocal folds, and as we have found in our breathing exercises, when we are anxious or stressed we tend to breathe from the upper-chest. This means that you will be unable to speak or hold a note for very long due to shortness of breath and tension in the body.

The spiritual level and the voice

The more you release holding patterns and expand your energy the more this will translate to the voice. Your voice will become richer, freer and greater in range. Ungrounded energy can manifest as a lot of air in the voice accompanied by high and floaty tones. As the energy system becomes balanced the tonal range of the voice will broaden. Rich tones appear and the voice sounds more grounded and less breathy.

Vocal warm-ups

Before working with the voice it is important that the vocal mechanism has been warmed up. This avoids damage to this delicate system. It is like any form of exercise, if you do not warm up properly you could sustain an injury. If the vocal folds crash together over a repeated length of time they can become hardened which can lead to inflexibility and calluses which are known as "nodules". It is unlikely that nodules will form through gentle toning but if you are planning a long voice session a few simple warm-ups before-hand will help you to look after your voice as well as allow the full range of your singing voice to reveal itself. Vocal warm-up exercises also help improve the quality of the voice as they act as a work-out for the vocal system. I can tell when my voice has not been properly warmed up as it is lacking in range and has a dry hissing quality to it. Before doing any voice work it is good to have a drink of water to lubricate the vocal folds. Tea, coffee and alcohol dehydrate the vocal mechanism so should ideally be avoided, but if you can't resist your morning latte then have a drink of water to flush the vocal folds before singing.

Exercise: Vocal warm-ups

Aim: The aim of these exercises is to gently warm the vocal folds before beginning your vocal wholing sessions.

Stand with the legs slightly apart or sit in a straight backed chair. Take slow and easy breaths from the solar plexus diaphragm and expand the breath into the vocal and pelvic diaphragms as you relax and settle in.

Beginning with an easy pitch in your upper range let out a sigh with an "AHH", sliding down to your lowest pitch. Repeat several times, gradually stretching your highest and lowest notes within comfortable limits.

Repeat this with "KAA", "SAA" and then "MAA"

Start with a low tone and sing "OOO", sliding up to a high pitch and down in the same breath. You will make a sound like a siren. Repeat this several times for a few minutes, gently extending your range.

The following check list is an at a glance reminder of important points to consider to be able to get the most from your sessions.

- Pay attention to your posture, tension in the body and diaphragms
- Check in on your breathing if you are breathing from the upper chest aim for the complete breath.
- Define the aim of your session and focus your intention
- Warm up your voice
- Get out of the way!

The first four points all require you to be present in the body but the final point seems to contradict the others. It is like learning to drive a car. In the beginning you need to think about all of the procedures that are involved, such as checking in the mirror before signaling and moving off, engaging the clutch before changing gear and determining the amount of pressure to put on the brakes to make a smooth stop. However, once these are mastered you are able to automatically perform each task seamlessly. In the iconic film *"Star Wars"*, Luke Skywalker is told by OB1 to *"use the force"* after failing to achieve a direct hit on the Death Star. He removes the visor which was helping him to make an accurate shot and "tunes in" to the force. Lo and behold a direct hit and Darth Vadar's Death Star is history! When first starting to work with the voice it can seem like rubbing your stomach and patting your head at the same time. Your mind is filled with things to remember, but once you have gone through the check list a few times you will be able to get out of the way and then the force will be with you!

(Humming) *"is the agent that helps to draw us into a profound state of quietude, relaxation and peace. Its comforting sound leads us deep within where we can find our true sense of self and therefore have great realisations and ideas."*
James D'Angelo

Humming

If the inhale is receiving from the universal flow and the exhale is giving, then humming is receiving and toning is giving. Closing the lips and internalizing the sound is a beautiful experience of giving to the self. OM is a balanced sound, being both giving and receiving. The "o" is the external expression of the sound and the "m" is the internalization of the sound.

By receiving unconditionally you free up any issues around receiving love, money, praise, success, good health, abundance and whatever else you desire. You are also able to give unconditionally and without resistance. If you have resistance to receiving from others this could be because of a core message to do with self-worth or an imbalance in the heart chakra. Humming can reinforce the love you have for yourself and, along with focused intention, can help you to free up any resistance around receiving.

Humming is also very good for issues around self-identity and boundaries as it helps you to feel who you are. As the vibrations of the voice are held within the body you can feel the sound reverberating inside you, bringing you to your center and giving yourself an internal sonic cuddle. If your energy is too expanded or overactive a few minutes of humming will bring yourself back into your body.

Exercise: Humming

Aim: To restore balance by feeding the inner realms through internalizing the vibration of your own sound.

Spend a few minutes humming. Practice singing in different pitches and feeling where they resonate in the body. When you have found a pitch that you resonate with stay with this for several minutes, humming into every area of your body and sending sonic cuddles within.

"Through toning the body has the opportunity to slip into and rest in our perfect pattern. It surrenders to the highest which the soul can direct the mind to imagine. In this the person finds peace and the answers to problems. His heritage of joy and wellbeing is claimed."
Laurelle Elizabeth Keyes

Toning

Toning is the singing of a single tone like a vowel or OM. It helps to relax and calm the system, slow the brainwave frequencies, respiration, heart rate and lower blood pressure. In her book *"Toning"* Laurelle, Elizabeth Keyes writes *one of the aids to healing which toning provides is the cleansing of the field"*. Singing words has a different effect on the system as the brain is more active because you are remembering the words and melody. The only exception to this is the singing of mantra which requires rhythmic repetition, allowing the brainwaves and the system to relax and calm. Toning allows you to get out of the way and align to the mind of God. During voice sessions it is not uncommon for people to say that they completely lost themselves in the process. Some people say that they feel as though they are "being sung". This happens when you are in resonance with the mind of God; the sound seems to move through you.

Aim to make your sounding sessions at least twenty minutes long if possible but if you need a quick boost use the sonic hot chocolate or sonic caffeine. You only need a few minutes to feel the benefit.

Sonic vitamins

These are very useful when you need a quick boost. They are like a sonic "power nap". The sonic vitamins can be added in to your sounding session or you can use them on their own. For example, you can start off with sonic hot chocolate to relax you before you start your full session. If you are doing a session in the morning you may like to finish with sonic caffeine to set you up for the day. If you are doing a session late in the evening and are feeling very energized you may like to finish with sonic hot chocolate to relax the system before sleeping.

Sonic caffeine

This exercise is perfect if you need a quick pick me up. You can use this in the morning to set you up for the day, or before a meeting or presentation when you need to be alert and focused. You can also use it when you are revising for exams as it stimulates the mental level. Sonic caffeine has been used to great effect with children with learning difficulties. I was conducting a piece of research into the use of sound to help improve learning ability and introduced the sonic caffeine exercise to a teacher I was working with. A few minutes of sonic caffeine really helped the children with learning difficulties to focus, especially before a maths class. She also used this sonic vitamin with children who had no learning difficulties to see what would happen. Some of the more hyperactive members of the class proceeded to bounce around the classroom both metaphorically (and almost literally!) for several minutes until the sonic hot chocolate was used. This class clearly did not require further stimulation! If your mental level is over stimulated or fatigued or you are in a state of anxiety try the sonic hot chocolate instead.

Exercise: Sonic caffeine

Aim: The aim of this exercise is to stimulate the energy system.

Spend a few moments toning EEE in a pitch that is comfortable for the voice but towards the top of your range. EEE is the sound of the crown chakra but the intention with this exercise is to stimulate the energy system and the mental level. If you place your hand on your head you can feel the effects of this vitamin in the head area. After a few moments stop and feel the buzz!

Sonic hot chocolate

This is perfect if you want to relax and if you need a sonic cuddle.

If you need to unwind at the end of a hard day or when you are stressed or over energized all you need to do is tone for a few minutes to achieve deep relaxation.

Exercise: Sonic hot chocolate

Aim: To relax the energy system.

Tone "AHH" in a pitch that is towards the lower end of your range for several minutes and bathe in the warmth of the relaxing vibrations as they move through the system. AHH is the sound of the heart chakra so it is easy to see why it gives you a warm sonic cuddle.

"The seven vowels, uniting in harmony, send forth a sound and glorify the world-builder"
The Gnostic Marcus

Sacred Vowels

The vowel sounds are non-linear and allow for expansion in the energy system whereas the consonants are the linguistic and energetic representation of contraction. If we didn't have vowels in our language we would communicate in hisses, tuts and clicks. Due to the expansive energy signature of the vowels they have long been thought of as sacred sounds. Musically the vowels produce the tone in our language and the consonants provide the percussive quality. Within tone is contained harmonics which also have a sacred quality to them. More about harmonics later.

The chakra sounds

The traditional Vedic system attributed Bija (seed) syllables to the chakras. In the West we use vowels and other sounds to massage the chakras. If you look around you will see that there are a few slightly different systems, but there is no right or wrong. Work with the system that resonates with you. Below I have listed the system that I work with. As you can see some of the sounds are not vowels. As new chakras have made themselves known I needed to find a sound that corresponded to the chakra. I found a sound for the thymus on the internet which worked really well and through meditation I have found a sound which seems to work very well with the energy of the Angel chakra. I use "NUR" for the Zeal point as the "N" sound resonates with this part of the skull and the harmonics within the tone are more identifiable, which reflects the transcendental nature of the Zeal point. The angel chakra seems to resonate very well with a "ZZZ" sound and the "UURR" brings in the audible harmonics. It is also interesting that some of the "newer" chakra sounds are those that encourage the use of audible harmonics when toned. Although all of the chakras have transcendental aspects, these newer chakra sounds seem to respond really well to sounds that enhance harmonics.

The Chakra Sounds

Chakra	Sound	
Base	ER	As in earth
Sacral	OO	As in booth
Solar Plexus	OH	As in dough
Heart	AHH	As in ask
Thymus	HUL	As in school, rather than hull. Divide the sound into half, concentrating 50 per cent on Huuuuu and 50 percent on lllll
Throat	EYE	As in eye, keep the sound open and avoid using too much eee at the end of the vowel
Zeal	NUR	As in manure. Feel the vibration in the zeal point area on the nnnnnn sound and curl the tip of the tongue upwards on the uuurrrr to create overtones.
Brow	AYE	As in hay. Keep the ay sound open and rounded for as long as possible and end on a small ee, rather than introducing to much eeeeeeeee
Angel	ZUR	As in azure. The ZZ sound keeps the energy in the head and the uurre creates the overtones.

Crown   EE   As in see. Feel the eeeee
                              resonating in the head

Exercise: Getting to know the chakra sounds

Aim: The aim of this exercise is to massage each chakra with its corresponding sound and to check for resonances.

Writing can distract the process so you may prefer to write this exercise up afterwards. If you are concerned that you won't be able to remember everything you experienced during your session, write about each chakra as you go or you can use a voice recorder if you prefer.

Starting at the base chakra, tone "ER" for a few minutes. Begin by focusing your attention on the base chakra for a minimum of three full toning breaths and then extend your awareness to all levels of being, toning "ER" a minimum of three times and scanning the whole system with this sound. Move to the next chakra, toning "OO", using the same system. You may find that each sound feels or sounds different depending on the center you are working on and you may feel drawn to change your pitch when you get to a certain center. Make a note of all of these differences to see if a pattern develops. Notice if you find it difficult to make sound, or if the sound feels "stuck" in some way. Also notice if you run out of breath when you are working on one chakra more than another or if you feel pain or tension in the physical body. Some sounds may trigger emotional release so you may feel tearful, angry or sad when you are focusing on a particular chakra. Note what you feel where. When you have finished tune into the levels of being as a whole and notice the difference. Is your physical level more relaxed? How is your emotional level? Is you mental level calmer? Does your energy feel expanded?

You can use this as a tool for self-diagnosis and a sonic massage for the chakras. Once you have moved through each chakra you can then go back and work on the chakras that showed up by spending a few minutes toning the corresponding chakra sound. You can also do a shorter version of this exercise by sweeping through the chakras in one breath from "ER" to "EE", repeating the sweep several times. This exercise is a wonderful "tune up" and can be used as needed but is a wonderful "sonic shower" first thing in the morning.

The chakra sounds and movement

I was introduced to the vowels and movement by Lorin Panny of *Tonalis* who teaches Eurythmy (amongst other things). Eurythmy is an expressive movement art developed by Rudolph Steiner. I have adapted the movements slightly and have added movements that work with the thymus, zeal and angel chakras. The chakra sounds move the body in a specific way. For the purpose of research I have done this exercise with groups of people in a completely blind study and it never fails to surprise me. I ask the group to close their eyes, tone a chakra sound, align to the sound and allow it the freedom to move their body. At a point during each sound and movement I ask the group to stop, hold their position and look around the room. Almost everyone is holding the same or very similar position! It is wonderful to see the sound working in this way as it confirms to me that the body is aligning to and sounding with the mind of God.

The benefits of working with sound and movement are many. Movement helps to transmute denser energy held at the physical level. By adding the energy of your movements into the sound you allow it to live in a way that the voice alone cannot do so if you require a more dynamic sounding session try the chakra sounds with movement. Be aware of your breathing and aim to breathe fully, freeing all of the diaphragms. Your session will then become a form of sonic Chi Gong and can be used to keep the physical body supple while moving energy throughout all of the levels of being. Forming a physical connection to the sound also deepens your relationship with all levels of your being. It is very possible that your brainwaves will not slow as much as if you were sedentary. However sometimes it is necessary to be more engaged in your sound work. Gentle movement enables you to stay present and yet still journey on the sound. This practice is perfect for use on a regular basis as part of your overall wholing program.

Exercise: The vowels and movement

Aim: The aim of this exercise is to move energy and sound through the physical body.

Spend time moving through each of the chakras from base to crown integrating sound, movement and the complete breath. Really feel each movement in the body and allow the sound to resonate deeply within. Is there a movement and/or sound that you found difficult? Make a note of where the sound or movement was 'stuck' or where you felt resistance and what it felt like. At the end of the full exercise, stop and allow the silence to flood in. Write up the exercise. If you can do this exercise every day over a period of time to see if a pattern develops and notice if the imbalances that have been highlighted are the same as with other exercises.

You can use this exercise as a whole Chi Gong exercise including all the chakras, or you can integrate the chakras that you most want to work on into a vocal session or at the beginning and/or end of a session with your instruments.

Chakras and Movement

Chakra	Sound	Movement
Base	ER	Knees soft and slightly bent, hands palm down to earth, visualize connection to Earth
Sacral	OO	Knees soft and slightly bent, bringing arms through

		treacle/warm chocolate, figure of eight with hips and arms. Visualize sensual energy
Solar Plexus	OH	Hugging self in a rounded way with arms (not tightly) stepping forward as your arms hug you. Visualize strengthening personal space
Heart	AHH	Hands on heart, opening slowly stepping backwards as your arms open, visualize opening to unconditional love
Thymus	HUL	Hands on thymus and send them forward, palms parallel. Visualize tunnel to the mind of God.
Throat	EYE	Palms starting off in prayer position. Turn right hand down to the ground and left hand up, slowly move the right arm down and the arm up, visualize a channel to heaven and earth
Zeal	NUR	Bringing the arms up to the Zeal point, palms facing the floor, elbows at the same height. Sweep the arms around at the level of the zeal in front and behind you in a sweeping circle stretching your awareness. Keep you knees soft and swivel slowly from the waist
Brow	AYE	Touch brow chakra as if to activate it and stretch arms

		forward and out to the sides seeing the path ahead
Angel	ZUR	Place hands in prayer position palms together at the level of the heart. Inhale and tone, taking the palms up to the angel. Rest the base of the hands on this chakra and imagine the sound going through your hands and connecting with the mind of God.
Crown	EE	Palms and arms parallel, starting at ground and stretching to the sky. Visualize cord to the center of the universe

As it is difficult to put movements into words, I have put the chakra movements on my website www.healthysound.com

The creation sounds of OM and HU

Both OM and HU are considered to be sacred as they *are* the sonic expression of the mind of God. In the Vedic teachings AUM is the cosmic sound, the *Pranava*. According to Swami Sivananda Radha, author of *"Mantras, Words of Power"* (when chanting the cosmic sound of AUM) *"spiritual practise or sadhana is not necessary, because one has truly become the Lord's property, the flute of Lord Krishna"*.

OM is the condensed version of AUM. AUM is the receptive principle and OM is more active. When constructing your sounding sessions you may like to choose which to use on the basis of your own energetic type. Do your nadis need balancing? If so you can use the active or receptive sounds of AUM and OM to bring balance and harmony. You can also see this in terms of constriction and release, with the AUM being more releasing and the OM more holding. Go with your intuition and see what feels best for you.

The AUM is in three parts, AH, OO and MM. The AH is the sound of the heart, the OO of the sacral (and therefore of creation) and the MM is the journey of the sound within ourselves. OM is in two parts, the OH of the solar plexus and the MM representing the journey within ourselves.

HU is the sound of God in the Sufi tradition. According to Hazrat Inayat Khan, *'the mystery of Hu is revealed to the Sufi who journeys through the path of initiation"*. HU is the essence of the creator; it is the sound of the still point from which everything else came. Interestingly it is very similar to the sound of the thymus chakra so perhaps the person who first found this sound tuned into the primordial sound of HU. You can tone these sounds for a whole session or combine them with other techniques and exercises in this book as and when it feels right. I like to use them at the beginning to set the space and at the end to finish, bringing the session full circle to completion.

Exercise: Vocal self-diagnosis

This exercise enables you to focus your sounding session on a particular area of the system that needs attention. The exercises in Part 1 may have given you a good idea of where your imbalances tend to be. You may also find that new areas show up during your sounding sessions as your energy system evolves and changes.

Symptoms can also resonate in a chakra that you were not expecting, so you may find that your headache is due to an imbalance in the base chakra rather than the brow.

Exercise: The drinking straw

Aim: The aim of this exercise is two-fold. You can use it as a tool for self-diagnosis by making a sweep of the energy system and locating areas of imbalance. You can also use this exercise as a form of sonic massage by repeating it for a minimum of five minutes, sweeping through the chakras several times.

Sit upright on a straight-backed chair. Imagine that your body is a hollow tube like a drinking straw. Begin to tone in a comfortable pitch using any vowel sound. Take your attention to the soles of the feet and as you tone visualize the sound being drawn through your body like liquid rising up the drinking straw. Notice if there are any areas where the voice gets stuck, wavers or cracks or if you find it difficult to move the voice past a certain point. You can repeat the exercise a couple of times to test if the imbalance still shows up in the same place. If it does you can use a chakra sound or other instrument to help to balance the area that has shown up. You can also use this technique as a form of sonic massage by continuing to bring' the voice through the body from feet to crown until the sound moves easily and smoothly through the chakras. When you start working with this exercise it is a good idea to repeat it every couple of days or so and write down what shows up. You may see a pattern developing which could tie in with your core messages and/or current state of health and wellbeing.

> *"Through self-observation, more presence comes into your*
> *life automatically"*
> Eckhart Tolle

Working With Your Divine Heart

In the chapter on the chakras I used an analogy of a castaway situation and mentioned the "love and power point" where a group has the opportunity to create paradise on Earth by transcending the solar plexus and coming from the heart. In the silver bowl that is our collective experience on this planet at this time perhaps we are at this point. The polarity between solar plexus and heart certainly seems to be growing and there are choices to be made. The more we work with the energy of the divine heart, the more our energy will entrain others, bringing people gently to the source. On the other hand perhaps this dimension will always need the "sinners" and the "saints". The light and shade of the human condition allows us to learn and grow. If we do not see our shadow how can we ever see our light? I don't have the answer, but what I do know is that by working with the divine heart you are able to experience a deep sense of self-love and connection, even when all around you seems to be in chaos.

Your Soul Sound

Many people say that your soul sound is something that you are born with and that it remains with you throughout your life. My experience of energy so far is that the only constant is change and therefore I believe that a healthy system is one that remains flexible and open to change. I have also noticed that over the years my soul sound has changed.

Your soul sound is the way you express yourself through sound at this time. It can also be used as your personal sonic vitamin. If you have issues around self-identity, expression and self-love, this is a really good sonic vitamin to use. It also helps to re-enforce the connection with all that is so is perfect if you feel disconnected from the mind of God.

Once you have identified your soul sound, spend five minutes or more toning at this pitch using any vowel sound or overtones that feel right. You can even conduct your chakra balancing sessions at this pitch going through each vowel in turn. If you choose this method make sure that you stay flexible and avoid getting stuck in your soul sound. Use a range of pitches during other exercises and check back periodically to see if your soul sound changes as you transmute the denser energy in the system.

Exercise: Finding your soul sound

Unless you possess perfect pitch you will need a chromatic tuner or keyboard for this exercise so that you can check your note. You can buy a chromatic tuner fairly cheaply from a music shop (more about purchasing a tuner can be found in the section on Himalayan bowls).

Aim: The aim of this exercise is to identify your soul sound.

Relax and spend time toning, changing the pitch until you settle on a note that resonates strongly with you. Avoid looking at the tuner while you are doing this exercise so that you don't influence the outcome of the experiment. When you have found your note, check the pitch and make a record of it. Repeat this exercise over a four week period and see if a pattern develops. If you find that more than one note shows itself, write your findings down and continue with the exercise until you settle on a note. You may feel that one note reflects your state of being more accurately than another. If you get a different reading during each session and are unable to decide which note is your soul note, put this exercise on the shelf for the moment and come back to it in a few weeks or more. It may be that you need to work through some of other exercises in this book first or you may not need to know your soul sound at this time.

Your heart song

The film *"Happy Feet"* features penguins that have a song which reflects their personality and they keep this throughout their life. Unlike the penguins in *"Happy Feet"* your heart song will change from session to session. This is a different technique to the soul sound exercise. Your heart song is a complete and spontaneous sounding of the mind of God through the heart center. It is also an alignment to bliss and an expression of self-love. Regular practice of this exercise is life-affirming, energy expanding and nurturing for the heart center It can also help with self-esteem, confidence and communication issues.

Exercise: Your heart song

Aim: To channel love through the heart center, open the heart center, align to love and reinforce self-love and self-esteem.

Put aside at least twenty minutes for this exercise. Begin by toning AUM or OM and when ready introduce a simple melody with no more than four notes in a complete breath. Don't think about what you are singing. The more you get out of the way the more you will be able to sound with the mind of God. If your mind stays too engaged it will encourage your brainwaves to stay in Beta rather than slip into Alpha or Alpha/Theta. Don't worry if the melody sounds discordant or strange at first as this is perfectly normal; you are getting used to the process. If you find yourself getting into performance mode ask the ego to step aside and bring your attention back to the heart chakra. Tone whatever comes from this center using a mixture of different vowel sounds. After this exercise spend time allowing the silence to flood in. Feel the sound in the body and notice if there are any resonances in the chakras or on any other level of being. It is also quite common to experience an emotional release during this exercise. Go with the flow and see what comes up. You can then use the exercises in Part 1 to identify and transmute any core messages that present themselves.

You can go deeper with this exercise if you sing in front of the mirror, sending unconditional love to yourself. If you have self-esteem, self-love or communication issues this exercise is perfect, but if you are in a vulnerable place, it is better avoided until you feel stronger as it can be very powerful. This exercise is not easy at first, but becomes easier with practice. As your awareness alters your face may take on a new appearance. Allow this process to happen naturally and with love. These images are beautiful and perfect aspects of you. If you feel uncomfortable at any time stop and do a grounding exercise (see the chapter on grounding).

Heart release

This exercise really helps to transmute anything held in the body on any level, but it is particularly good for releasing anything held on the emotional level as well as physical pain. If you feel physically or emotionally hurt or are feeling the effects of negatively charged energy in the system you can release this by toning "AHH" whilst visualizing the pain or imbalance coming out of the body on the voice. When you first start doing this exercise give yourself five minutes maximum and make sure that you warm your voice up beforehand as it can be very powerful. As you become more accustomed to this exercise you can extend the time as necessary. You can also work on past events bringing them to mind, feeling the resonance in the body and toning them out. Take care not to strain the voice with the force of the emotion you are releasing. You may find that the sound you make is discordant or dull at the beginning and becomes lighter and brighter at the end of the session. This is due to the the the denser energy being released from the system. During this exercise you may find that you also release certain emotions along with the toning, such as tears or laughter. When you are ready to bring this exercise to a close spend a few moments giving yourself a sonic cuddle with a heart song or an AHH with a loving intention towards yourself.

"The generation of an infinite spiral of harmonious overtones, tuning in to the infinite, or focussing on the natural harmonies of the world around us, or the orbs of the heavens, or even the building blocks of matter itself may be the key to unlocking the door to the great powers and influences that surround us."
Peter Galgut

Overtones - Creating a Sonic Rainbow

Most musical instruments create harmonics when they are played. When you pluck a string the sound you hear contains other sounds known as "partials", "overtones" or "harmonics". Sounds that have fewer harmonics, such as the crystal bowls, are considered to be "purer" in tone.

Sounds with multiple frequencies such as glass breaking, waves crashing on a beach, gongs and cymbals contain complex frequencies, making it harder to define a fundamental tone (although you can get gongs that are tuned). Himalayan singing bowls are also rich in harmonics as they contain many different metals each with its own fundamental frequency.

When an instrument is played a particular set of frequencies is produced which is the "sound signature" "timbre" or "color" of the instrument. It is this that allows us to identify the instrument that is being played. For example, if an oboe and a flute both play a middle C it is still easy to tell the two notes apart because an oboe sounds different from a flute due to its construction.

This discovery was to revolutionize music forever, transforming it from art (which was considered by some at that time to be an indulgence) to a science.

Pythagoras rushed home and began making an instrument that would enable him to explore this new world of harmonics in greater depth and came up with the "monochord".

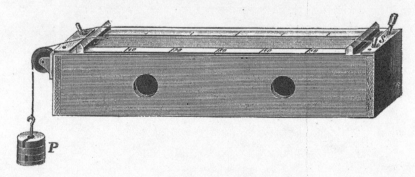

A Monochord

A monochord is a long wooden box with one string stretched between two points. The string is raised from the surface of the box by a moveable bridge which allows the string to be divided. When the string is plucked the sound waves travel back and forth rather like waves hitting the sea shore. As the sound-waves collide with each other they create new shorter waves which have higher sounds. When you pluck the string you will hear the fundamental tone of the "open" string. When you divide the string with a finger, bridge or other divider and pluck either the left or right side you will hear different tones that are mathematically related to the fundamental tone. It is rather like a rainbow. If you hold a prism up to the sunlight it will divide the light into the colors of the rainbow just as the whole string divides into sonic partials of itself.

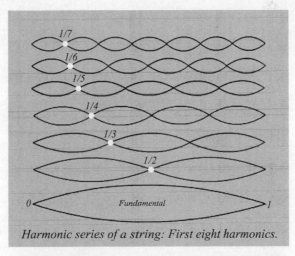

Harmonic series of a string: First eight harmonics.

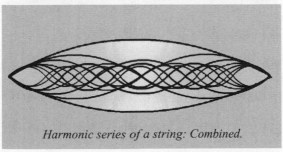

Harmonic series of a string: Combined.

The Harmonic Series

Due to the divisional nature of harmonics once a sound is made the harmonics continue to divide into higher and higher frequencies, travelling from the originator of the tone to infinity. No sound is ever lost. Every word you have spoken or song you have sung will resonate throughout the universe forever. The above diagram illustrates the relationship that the harmonics have to the fundamental tone. Harmonics are a sonic rainbow stretching across space and time containing a wealth of information about the originator of the sound and resonating with other sounds and frequencies within the mind of God.

In 1814 Josef von Fraunhofer discovered that there were a series of black lines contained within a rainbow. These lines (now known as Fraunhofer lines) contain information that comprises the periodic table of elements used by scientists today. I believe that just as there is information contained within the light spectrum, there is information contained in the sound spectrum. Harmonics have long been associated with producing an altered state and the fact that the sound goes on forever has contributed to them being known as a "stairway to the divine". My experience is that they certainly create a different energy when they are being used in a therapeutic or transformational way. By tapping into the information contained in the sound spectrum you are sounding the mind of God and therefore a wealth of knowledge becomes available to you. This is what makes working with sound so special, so powerful and yet so simple.

Stairway to heaven

Harmonic singing (also known as overtone singing and throat singing) is found in different parts of the world. The most well-known form of overtone singing originates from Mongolia and is known as "Khoomei" (also spelt Khoomii and Xhoomii). The Mongolian techniques produce a range of sounds from high and bright to deep and dark. The technique allows the singer to produce more than one note at once, the fundamental tone and one or more harmonics.

Overtones were traditionally sung to imitate and connect with the sounds and forces of nature, to worship the nature spirits and to ward off evil. In Tuva overtones were sung to imitate the sound of the wind coming from the mountains or sunrays as they hit the grasslands. In Mongolia overtones were sung to imitate the sounds of the mythical river Eev, which was said to have magical properties. Khoomei has also been known as the *"voices echo"* or *"birds echo"* as some birds create overtones when they call.

The Tibetan Gyuto monks have the "one voice chord" which is a rich, deep and dark sound. Rather than being taught, this technique is passed from teacher to student by osmosis. I had experience of this when I attended the popular Mind, Body and Spirit exhibition in London. My exhibition booth was almost opposite another sound therapist and performer, Nestor Kornblum. Throughout the weekend we created a wonderful sound bubble between us. We had a great time "bowling", chanting, overtoning, drumming and didgeridooing our way through the show! At times Nestor would sing in the Khargyraa style of Khoomii which is a deep dark style that I loved. When I had a spare moment I stood in front of him while he sang, bathing in the wonderful sound.

A few months later I was giving a workshop in Finland. My colleague Linda and I had just finished a long and wonderful day of sound and were enjoying a traditional Finnish sauna in a little lodge on the edge of a lake. We were toning and overtoning and all of a sudden the deep Khargyraa sound emerged from my throat! I was very grateful to Nestor for transferring the knowledge to me. Although I was able to sing in this style my technique did not feel fully integrated. A little while later I was working with sound practitioners and teachers Jonathan Cope, Rami Shaafi and Colin Goring, who could all sing in the Khargyraa style. I explained that I didn't feel that my Khargyraa did not feel fully integrated. They embraced me in a big hug and began overtoning. My body resonated strongly with the vibration of their wonderful Khargyraa sandwich! A few days later my Khargyraa was back and it's been with me ever since. Thank you all for teaching me this technique. If you want to learn Khargyraa (or any other style), then I suggest you sit with as many good singers as possible!

Although I can sing this style I do not consider myself to be a Mongolian overtone singer. The Mongolian techniques require study and many years of practice. As a sound practitioner I concentrate on Western style overtone singing which is a softer, easier to learn style that is kinder to the vocal mechanism when singing for long periods of time.

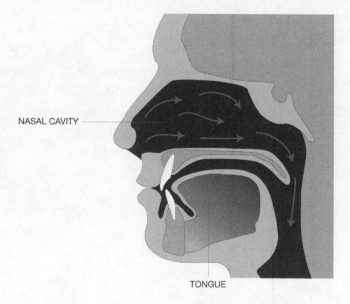

The Resonating Cavities

The chest, throat, mouth, nasal and paranasal cavities are our resonating chambers which add color and richness to the voice. Think "duvet" and "bathroom". If you were to sing under the duvet the softness of the fabric would absorb your voice and all of the subtleties and harmonics in the voice would also be lost. If you were to go into the bathroom and sing your voice would come pinging back to you and you may even hear the subtle overtones contained within the voice.

Within the mouth your resonating chambers are the bathroom and your tongue is the duvet. When producing harmonics you use the tongue in a specific way to allow the harmonic to be divided from the fundamental just as Pythagoras divided the string of his monochord, allowing the harmonic to be heard. As well as using the tongue you also use the resonating chambers within the mouth. There are several different sound shapes that you can make with the voice to enable the harmonics to be heard. Here are a few to start you off, but feel free to explore with your own sounds.

EEE-OOOO

Sing an "EEE" in mid-range. Keep the back of the tongue flattened against the back of the top teeth but don't force it. You need some tension, but not too much. Now move from "EEEE" to "OOOO" keeping the tongue in the same position but moving the lips. You may hear the harmonics emerge. Try this several times really squeezing the sound over the top of the tongue. You may find that by moving the tip of the tongue very slightly you are able to hear even more overtones popping out.

AWWREE

Sing an "AW" (oar) sound and send the sound up the back of your nose, adding a nasal quality to the voice as much as you can. A good tip with this is to put your hand in front of your mouth. If you are singing through your nose there will be less vibration and air hitting the palm of your hand than if you are singing through your mouth.

The tongue will drop to the bottom of the mouth when you sing an "AW" giving you plenty of space in the mouth. You can get an even better mouth shape if you imagine you have a hot potato in your mouth and you are drawing in air over the potato to cool it down but keep the lips fairly open (so that you can get your finger easily in between them) this will give you a good mouth shape. Then begin to bring the "REE" sound in slowly. The jaw will slowly begin to close and the tongue will flatten out. Squeeze the "REE" sound slowly and deliberately over the top of the tongue, still sending the tone up the back of the nose.

MEEEOOOO

Start off humming "MMM" with the mouth closed, imagining the sound coming out of the nose. Open the lips slightly and move the lips from "EEE" into the "OOO" position.

NUUUURRR

This is the sound for the zeal point. Start off with the "NNN" sound, still sending the sound up the nose and then begin to bring the "UUURRR" sound in. Move the tip of the tongue slowly up and down to alter the harmonics.

GONG, GUNG, GANG, GING

This exercise is good for hearing the harmonics change with the different sounds. Sing "GONG GONG GONG" moving to "GUNG GANG" and "GING" as necessary. This helps to build muscle memory in the mouth and tongue and helps you to tune into the harmonics in the voice. You can also do this with "MEE","MOO" and "MAA".

Once you have mastered these different overtone producing techniques you are then able to improve your technique, taking off the consonants and smoothing off the edges until you have a sound which is purer in harmonics without the "attack" of the MMM, NNN or G.

Exercise: Climbing the stairway to heaven

Aim: The aim for this exercise is to travel on the sound current of your own harmonics. Once you are familiar and competent with the overtoning techniques and don't have to think too hard about creating overtones you are in the perfect place to be able to get out of the way and enjoy the process.

Begin toning for as long as it feels right until you feel you are moving into a relaxed state of being. Then bring the overtones in for the rest of the session. Note down any resonances that you feel on the levels of being and in the chakras.

"If you ask a lama with a singing bowl in his hands, whether it is true that they are used for psychic, psychological and physical purposes, he will smile and reply: 'Perhaps'."
Joska Soos

Himalayan Singing Bowls

I found the above quote by the Hungarian shaman Joska Soos in Eva Rudy Jansen's book '*Singing Bowls*' and it perfectly illustrates the mystery that surrounds these wonderful tools. This air of secrecy has fascinated people since the first travelers ventured into the Himalayan region and heard "the bowls that sing". They are more commonly known as Tibetan singing bowls, but as they have been made in Bhutan, Nepal, India and Tibet perhaps a more accurate name for them is "Himalayan singing bowls".

We know that sound has been used for thousands of years in prayer, worship and other sacred practices. Before the Bronze age sacred instruments were made from wood, stones, bone, shells and animal skins but as metal tools started to be crafted, so did instruments. It is thought that the singing bowls are related to the bell and gong. The use of gongs and bells in sacred practices can be traced back several thousand years. In Japan bells were (and still are) placed at the entrance to a temple or shrine to call on the Gods, and gongs have been used to ward off evil spirits and call on good spirits for at least four thousand years.

The bowls are either struck gently or played by running a stick, or wand as I prefer to call it, around the rim allowing the bowl to sing. The ancient bowls contained many different metals, some say as many as nine were used but the most common number of metals was seven, corresponding to the seven planets of old (which were the seven planets visible to the naked eye).

Metal	Planet	Chakra
Gold	Sun	Solar Plexus
Silver	Moon	Sacral
Iron	Mars	Solar Plexus
Copper	Venus	Heart
Tin	Jupiter	Brow
Lead	Saturn	Base

According to Frank Perry legend also says that metallic tektites (meteorites) found on the mountains were also added to the mix to reinforce the connection between heaven and earth.

The exact combinations of these metals are not known and would probably have depended on the ore that was available in each region as well as what could be obtained from traders. It is possible that different makers had their own combinations of metals that they liked to use as well as the style of bowl they preferred to make. There may also have been different styles for each region or maker. Harmonics have a big part to play in the sacredness and effectiveness of these bowls as a therapeutic tool.

Each metal has a different resonant frequency. When the seven metals in the bowl begin to sing sound that is produced is rich in harmonics, which we know alters our brainwaves and raises consciousness. Each singing bowl has its own color, shape and personality and no two Himalayan bowls are the same, even if they are the same size. The traditional way of making the bowls was to hand hammer them, each dent and mark on the surface of the bowl adding personality and color to the sound. Just as the ancient swords were infused with prayers and intention with the blow of the hammer, so perhaps were the bowls. Decorations were often added afterwards which may reflect the intention of the maker or signify the use of the bowl. Some bowls were made to offer protection and some have sacred symbols and mantras engraved or painted on the outside, allowing the message to travel on the sound-wave when the bowl is played; rather like a sonic prayer flag. The thickness and shape of the bowl also plays a part in the sound that the bowl makes. If you compare two bowls of the same size, one with a thicker rim and one with a thinner rim, the bowl with the thicker rim will be higher in tone. The thinner rimmed bowls will tend to be deeper, but can sound tinny if the rim is too thin.

As well as the therapeutic properties of the sound it has also been documented that eating out of the bowls gave the consumer a homeopathic dose of the metals, and that women who had just given birth were required to eat out of them for one month. As these bowls contain lead and mercury, I am not sure whether I would be comfortable with eating out of them!

Choosing your bowl

There are many places where you can buy Himalayan singing bowls but good quality antique singing bowls are becoming harder to find. It does not mean that you will not find a real treasure hiding in a shop or exhibition somewhere, but if it is important to you to have an antique singing bowl find a reputable place to buy one. It is

Choosing a Himalayan Singing Bowl

lovely to have a bowl with history, but as a sound practitioner the sound is more important to me than the story behind the bowl. If you are on a limited budget you can find contemporary singing bowls that are made with a loving intention and sound wonderful. Be prepared to shop around. I am always on the look out to find the best bowls I can for my students and to pass on to others at workshops and exhibitions. I have several good suppliers who buy their bowls ethically and I trust their sources. When a shipment of bowls arrives I go and play every bowl, which sometimes runs into hundreds (I *love* my job!). I tune into each bowl's song and choose the sweetest, most beautifully sounding bowls that I can.

Often your bowl will choose you and therefore you may find a bowl calling you. Listen to this as it may be a bowl that could help you to reach a new level of being. Sometimes you may be drawn to the dirtiest, grumpiest bowl lurking in a dark forgotten corner somewhere; one that literally says "go away!" when you pick it up. If you feel a tugging at your heart-strings and are unable to put it down perhaps it is for you.

If you are intending to work with one bowl choose with your heart, but if you are looking for more than one or a full chakra set you may find it useful to have a chromatic tuner to enable you to choose bowls of different notes. You can buy a tuner from a music shop or online. Make sure it is one that has an external microphone and ideally one that shows you how many "cents" the tone is from perfect pitch. If you are interested in working with octaves, you may like to choose a tuner that also registers the octave. When choosing your bowl you can either choose one to resonate with a particular chakra to reflect your soul sound, or choose completely with your heart and go for the bowl that calls you. If you are continually drawn to bowls of the same note it may be that you need that particular sonic vitamin or it that the bowl corresponds to the chakra that you are working on at the moment. You may like to choose a bowl that resonates with your soul sound or one that sits comfortably within your vocal range so you can tone along with it.

If I am on a shopping trip to find a bowl to work with a specific chakra I will take my tuner with me, otherwise I will leave it at home and choose with my heart. Be aware that by doing this you can end up with several bowls of the same note. I've done this myself. When I am meditating with my Himalayan bowls I usually choose a few from my collection to play but every now and again I play them all in one long sitting. During one of these sessions I found that many of my bowls were the same pitch. I had collected them independently of each other over a number of years. I checked my tuner and they were A#. Guess what my soul note is.....you've got it, A#! Even though I have several bowls of the same note each one has a different personality. Even though the Himalayan bowls are rich in harmonics there will be a fundamental tone that you can use to determine the overall frequency. This is the lowest or more predominant tone when the bowl is played. Other wands and beaters may bring out different tones, so you may find a bowl that you can use for several different purposes by playing it in different ways (see "Playing Your Bowl").

Before you go bowl shopping hold any intention that you have for working with your bowl in your mind as this will help the right bowl to be drawn to you. It could be that you are looking for a bowl to help you relax or for use in meditation or that you are looking for a space-clearing bowl or stimulating bowl. Lower tones tend to relax as they have a lower frequency and therefore a slower sound-wave and higher tones stimulate. I have a few high frequency Himalayan bowls in my collection which are very good for space-clearing and stimulating the system.

When you choose a bowl hold it in your hands and tune in to its energy before you start to play it to see how it feels. After a few moments begin to play the bowl. Is it easy to play? Hold it to one ear and then the other, close your eyes and tune deeply into its song. How does it sound and feel? Move the bowl around your body as you play. Is your energy system interacting with the sound? It can be really helpful to ask someone else to play it for you so that you can tune into the bowl. Each person will affect the sound of the bowl they are playing in a subtle way as their energy interacts with the bowl so make sure you spend at least a few minutes playing the bowl yourself as well. Then take a good look at the bowl. If it is very old it can be fairly patinated and may have hairline cracks. Small cracks are not ideal although they can be mended. If the cracks are not too big and do not affect the sound they should not present a problem. Two of my favorite bowls have small cracks in them and they sing beautifully! The most important thing to look for is an even rim. If the rim is oxidized or dented it may affect the playing quality of the bowl, although small dents and imperfections are not an issue as they can be polished out and oxidization should not be a problem if it can be removed with a granulated metal polish. Seek advice from someone who works with metal or a specialist in antiques if you are at all concerned. You may also see markings and writing on the bowl, which adds further character and history and may give you an idea of where it came from and what it has been previously used for. Some less scrupulous bowl sellers have realized that engraved bowls can command a higher price and add writing and symbols to the bowls. If you come across a bowl with markings have a good look and see if the patina inside the markings matches the outside surface of the bowl. If the surface inside the marking is very shiny I would ask lots of questions before handing over your money or you may be happy with markings that have been added at a later date. I have a couple of old bowls with more contemporary markings, but they have been done well and to me they add to the character and story of the bowl.

Playing your bowl

Balance your bowl on the palm of your non-dominant hand. Cup your hand slightly but make sure that your fingers don't wrap around the sides of the bowl as this will inhibit the sound. If your bowl is too big to hold you may prefer to place it on a mat, ring or cushion which will hold your bowl steady whilst you play. Take the wand in your dominant hand and begin to run it around the rim of the bowl in a clockwise direction. Playing clock-wise has the feeling and intention of sending the sound outwards from the bowl and playing anti-clockwise brings the sound inwards. If you are left handed you may prefer to reverse this. Try both and see which one feels right to you. If you are holding the bowl in your hand you will feel a slight vibration as the bowl begins to sing. Keep winding the wand around the bowl and take it away when a sufficient volume has been reached and before the wand begins to rattle against the bowl (which is a sign that it is being overplayed). Allow the bowl to sing. Put the wand back after a few moments to keep the sound going.

If you would like to play in a more gentle sustained way run the wand around the rim a little more slowly than before keeping it in constant contact with the bowl. If the wand begins to rattle against the bowl slow the wand down, use slightly more pressure or take it away from the bowl. You can limit the amount of vibration by using a wand made from a softer wood or one that is covered in suede, leather or vinyl. Experiment with a range of different wands as each one will bring out different tones and sounds from the bowl. A softer wand tends to bring out the deeper tones and a harder wand the higher tones. Also experiment with the playing position. Playing with the wand on the rim at a 45 degree angle may isolate a higher harmonic whilst playing with your wand more parallel to the side of the bowl may bring out lower, richer harmonics.

Experiment with the sound by putting your mouth close to the rim or side of the bowl while it is singing. Open and close your mouth like a goldfish but don't make a sound. Allow the cavity of the mouth to manipulate the sound of the bowl. There may be a point when you hear a "wah wah wah" sound. If you can't hear it move the bowl around as the hammering on the surface of the bowl will create "hot spots" where the wah wah will become apparent. Some bowls produce a wah wah easier than others so don't be disheartened if your bowl doesn't make this sound. It will give you a good reason to buy another!

Fountain and water bowls

Some bowls are known as "fountain" or "water" bowls. If your bowl has a line running around the inside it may be a fountain bowl. Fill the bowl with water up to the line and play. If the water fizzes and little spouts or fountains spring forth you have a fountain bowl! Some bowls produce wonderful plaintive cries. Fill your bowl with a few centimeters of water, start the bowl singing, take the wand away and make circles with the bowl in your hand so that the water climbs the insides of the bowl rather like brandy in a glass when it is being warmed. The action of the water circulating in the bowl will alter the sound that the bowl is making allowing it to make a wonderfully haunting cry.

Talking bowls

A talking bowl makes a talking sound when it is rocked back and forth on the palm of the hand. Hold your bowl on a flat hand when it is singing and gently tip the bowl back and forward. You may hear it making a sound rather like a wah wah.

Lingham bowls

These are very rare and they don't always produce the best sound. They can be fairly thick sided and have a raised prominence in the center which is the lingham (male sexual organ). This bowl was traditionally played by the male elder of a village. In some instances sacrifices were made and the blood of an animal placed inside the lingham bowl. This could possibly be to do with fertility and is very likely to be linked to the animist/shamanistic Bon traditions.

Protection bowls

There are some bowls which have markings around the rim which are like circles with a dot

A Lingham bowl

in the middle. Some people say they are like eyes and that bowls with markings like these are warding off the evil eye. Others say they are supposed to be sequins and are just another form of decoration. If you find one of these bowls, play it and see if the bowl tells you its story.

Chama bowls

Chama bowls are very rare and have an interesting sound quality to them. Dated at approximately 17th century they have very thick sides and a rim that is smaller than their belly. Their shape seems to indicate that they may have been made

Chama Bowls

in Bhutan, as Bhutanese bowls tend to have a flatter base. They often have one or two lines a few centimeters from the top of the outside of the rim. They are also made from a combination of metals but their sound is unlike other Himalayan bowls in that they have a very pure focused sound which is almost crystalline in nature.

Magic happens when more than one Chama bowl is played at the same time. As the sounds of the bowls combine beat frequencies, bell-like ringing tones, warbles and other wonderful consciousness altering sounds emanate from these wonderful bowls. I have spent many hours playing the bowls and have found that they are very good for expanding the energy field. Their effects are similar to, but not as powerful as, the Peruvian whistling vessels which have been called *"sonic ayahausca"*. I won't be covering the whistling vessels in this book but if you feel drawn to finding out more about these powerful tools there is an article on my website or Daniel Statnekov's book *"Animated Earth"* is a good source of information.

A Japanese Singing Bowl

Japanese bowls

The Japanese singing bowls are smooth, high sided bowls which are similar in shape to a Chinese tea bowl. They are made in Japan and Nepal and are usually machine turned or cast and therefore are smooth on the inside and out. They are generally made from a fewer number of metals and their wall thickness is very even so their sound is purer with fewer harmonics. Their sound can be higher in pitch and can produce a focused and almost crystalline sound. This makes them very good for space-clearing and are stimulating rather than relaxing. In Japan they are played by striking them on the outside while chanting or saying prayers but you can also play them in the same way as the Himalayan bowls are played.

Whenever I travel I take an instrument with me. In 1997 I travelled to Japan and took a small Bhutanese bowl with me. I was staying with a Japanese family who had both Buddhist and Shinto shrines in their house. Sitting on a cushion in front of the shrine to the Buddha was a small Japanese bowl. I couldn't speak Japanese and they couldn't speak English so I was thrilled to find an opportunity for communication beyond words. I ran up to my room to get my beloved little travelling bowl and wand. When I returned I proudly showed them my bowl and began to play. They looked at me open mouthed as if they'd never seen anything like it before. After a few circuits on my bowl I realized that all was not going to plan. I thought that perhaps I had unintentionally offended them in some way.

The couple spoke to each other in Japanese and then ran to the kitchen and started rifling through the kitchen drawers. A few minutes later they came back with a thick wooden spoon and proceeded to try to play their Japanese bowl with the handle of the spoon! After a lot of hilarity and some Jap-English I finally understood that the Japanese strike their bowls when they play them and that they had never seen a bowl played in such a way before. From then on I could see by the hand signals that I was being introduced to everyone I met as the *"girl who plays her bowl by running the stick around the edge"*!

Care of your bowls

The more you treat your sacred tools with respect and reverence the more they will reward you. I personally like all of my bowls to be wrapped and tucked snugly up when they are not being used. This is also for practical reasons as some of the antique bowls can be quite brittle and can crack if they are dropped or knocked hard. As well as the practical reasons for wrapping them up it also shows your respect for your sacred therapeutic tools. You can get some lovely cloths and bags which will protect your bowls and enable you to transport them more easily. If you have bowls ranging in size you can you can also stack them inside each other Russian doll style for easy transportation.

When you first get your bowl you may like to cleanse it. There is a range of good space clearing mists available. You can use a Harmonia Space Mist (there is one specifically for cleansing Himalayan bowls) an Aura Soma quintessence or you can smudge them with sage or incense if you prefer. You can also make up your own blend, use prayer, water from a holy well or some people place them on a large amethyst bed.

I had just bought a lovely Himalayan bowl which resonated with the heart chakra and was driving home across Dartmoor in the pouring rain. I spotted a small stone circle close to the road and pulled the car over to have a look. Behind one of the small standing stones was a pool of water deep enough to fully cover my new bowl. I placed the bowl into the pool and watched as it was bathed in the rainwater charged with the energy of the sacred site. I'm convinced that it had more of a glow when it came out!

It is not advisable to scrub your bowl with brass polish or any chemicals as by cleaning away the patina, you would be cleaning away hundreds of years of history. The most common way of determining the age of a bowl is by the patina and if this is not intact it can be difficult to tell the age of a bowl but if you are ok with this and prefer to have a shiny bowl, go with whatever feels right for you.

Exercise: Getting to know your Himalayan bowl

Aim: The aim of this exercise is to connect with the sound signature of your bowl

After your bowl has been cleansed spend time examining it and meditating with it without playing. Feel the energy coming from the bowl and allow your energy to blend with the energy of the bowl and vice versa. Do you get any images or feelings from the bowl?

Now begin playing the bowl. Feel the energy of the bowl on the palm of your hand. Your palm chakras will be interacting with the sound and may activate, making your hands feel warm and tingly. Play for several minutes getting to know the character and energy of the bowl. Is it a lively or relaxed sound? Is it warm and soft or cold and penetrating? Does it have a message for you or give you an idea as to what it would like to be used for? After a minimum of twenty minutes of interacting with your bowl stop and feel its sound in your body. Notice how you feel on all levels of being and write up anything that has come up during this session.

Exercise: Sonic massage
Aim: The aim of this exercise is to give your system a sound massage with the Himalayan bowl.

Hold the bowl and run it up and down the midline of your body level with your chakras. If there is a chakra that you would like to work with, hold the bowl level with this center and spend a few moments concentrating the sound in this area. Continue playing the bowl and moving it slowly up and down the body. Notice any resonances in the system, breathe into them and release with a sigh on "AHH"! Keep playing if you can, you can always go back and re-process this imbalance later if it is still with you at the end of the session.

Keep playing until you feel you need to stop. Then spend time holding and playing the bowl in a comfortable position so you can drift away on the sound. Tune in to all your levels of being and note down anything that comes up for you. When you have finished and do a grounding exercise if necessary.

Sometimes the sound will resonate with an injury or you may feel tension in the neck and shoulders due to stress or another cause. Sometimes when we relax our mental level we are drawn to areas of physical tension in the body that the adrenaline had previously hidden from our awareness. It is only when we stop that we are often drawn to the imbalances in our system. We know that by becoming still we are able to hear the mind of God speaking to us.

You may feel the sound has activated one or more of your chakras or you may see color, feel hot, cold, tingling or buzzing. You may be transported to another place or time or have memories that you believe may be from a past life. Whatever you feel, listen to the messages within these experiences and don't worry if they don't mean anything to you at this time. It doesn't really matter; it is the listening that counts.

Exercise: Sonic symphony

Aim: The aim of this exercise is to feel how the different sounds and energy of the bowls interact with your system.

Take two or three Himalayan bowls and a selection of wands. The experience you have gained from your usual sounding sessions will have given you a good idea how each bowl interacts with your system. If you have a large number of bowls, choose the appropriate bowls to fit the intention of your session. If you only have two or three, use all three.

Set your space in the way that suits your needs and the intention for the session. Some people light candles and/or incense and wear clothing that is reserved for their sounding sessions, but do what feels right for you. Acknowledge your bowls and set them out in front of you in a sacred and respectful way.

Choose a lower toned bowl to play first as this will relax the brainwaves and allow the system to become more receptive. After a few minutes move between the different bowls taking time to play each one. Feel the resonances in the system as each bowl interacts with your energy in its own way.

This is a lovely work-out for the energy system and helps you to identify resonances that may not have previously shown themselves.

"They produce a sound and effect that is out of this world. In all my work with acoustic and electronic instruments, including Japanese and Tibetan bowls, these quartz bowls represent a unique and extraordinary resource."

Steven Halpern

Crystal Bowls

The frosted crystal bowls were originally made for the semi-conductor industry; they are used to grow quartz wafers for microchips. The bowls are made from 99 per cent quartz sand which is gathered from seams under the earth. The sand is placed into a centrifugal mould which is spun, forcing the sand to the outer edge of the mould.

Crystal Bowls

At a certain point an electric charge of around 4,000 degrees is fired into the mould which fuses the quartz instantly into a bowl. You could say the bowls are born with a big bang, much like our universe!

The semi-conductor industry orders large quantities of these bowls which are known to them as *"silica growth crucibles"*. Sometimes the odd contaminant appears in the bowl (you may notice a black dot or small mark). These bowls cannot be used by the semi-conductor industry and are therefore rejected. These rejected bowls are bought by companies supplying the sound therapy community. Unless you are intending to grow quartz wafers in your bowl a small mark should not make any difference and won't affect the sound or energy of the bowl. Personally I like seeing the marks as it adds character. If purity is a concern for you the quartz that a crystal bowl is made from is purer than most regular quartz points you can buy in a crystal shop.

Frosted crystal bowls are clear bowls with a granulated surface. The frosting gives the bowl an opaque finish and is very useful as it helps you to grip your bowl when you are moving it around. Clear quartz bowls are made by extruding molten quartz to form a tube which is then cut and blown into a bowl shape by a glass blower. Clear bowls are considered to be more fragile as they are thinner than the frosted bowls and as a result are currently made to a maximum of 12 inches (approx 30 centimeters). The clear bowls come with round or flat bottoms. Both can be hand held as well as placed on a rubber ring. The round-bottomed bowls sit so well in the hand. They are perfect for sonic massage but need a deep ring or cushion to sit on when they are not being held. A small clear bowl is a real asset to any sound-workers tool-kit as it is light enough to be tucked inside a back-pack when travelling. If you'd like to work with sacred sites, I recommend one of these.

Different types of crystal bowl are now being made to meet the growing demand. There are colored bowls and some which have other crystals such as rose quartz or amethyst added to them. Some of the colored bowls have mineral dyes added to the quartz producing bright colors. There are also bowls which have had precious metals such as gold and platinum added to the quartz. Usually this is fused to the surface of the bowl producing wonderful rainbow pink, gold and purple hues. There are also "practitioner" bowls which have a handle that enables you to direct the sound to where it is needed. These bowls are also good for space-clearing as you can get into all of the corners in a room more easily. Some of the handles of these bowls contain crystals; some are hollow and some are solid. I designed the "infinity bowl" which is a dumbbell shaped practitioner bowl with a bowl at each end of the handle. These wonderful bowls enable you to play a sustained interval which you can move within the field and they look and sound fabulous! There is no right or wrong when choosing a crystal bowl. It is all down to personal preference. It is worth shopping around to find exactly what suits your needs.

The sound signature of a crystal bowl is very different from any other instrument as they produce an almost perfect sine-wave, which is a pure sound that has few harmonics. Some of the clear bowls do produce harmonics due to the manufacturing technique producing a slightly uneven wall thickness which adds a lovely quality to the crystalline sound. People often describe the crystal bowls as being "ethereal", "otherworldly", "angelic", "cool", "linear", "astral" and "extra-terrestrial".

We know that denser imbalances can have smaller more resistant energy patterns which can be harder to transmute. The pure, sustained tones of the crystal bowls create space within your sounding session and allow you to reach a deep and expanding state of being.

Choosing your bowl

Choosing a crystal bowl is a very similar process to choosing a Himalayan bowl. You may like to choose a crystal bowl that corresponds to the chakra you are working with or one that resonates with your soul sound. If you are lucky enough to find a supplier that has several bowls ask if they don't mind if you spend time playing the bowls before you make your decision or you may prefer to order online and trust that you will receive the right bowl for you at this time. You may like to choose a note that is different from your Himalayan bowl if you have one so that you are expanding the range of frequencies you can use during your wholing sessions.

Cleansing your bowl

When you first get your bowl you may like to give it what I call a "major cleanse". The intention behind this process is to remove any residual energy within the bowl that does not serve its new purpose. I see it rather like wiping the hard-drive of a computer.

As we have already explored intention is key, so it is important to go with whatever cleansing process or ritual that resonates with you. Below is the method I like to use.

Prepare a bowl cleansing solution by filling a bath with enough water to completely cover your bowl or bowls. Add several handfuls of sea salt crystals to the water and stir to make sure all the crystals have dissolved. You can add water which contains a chosen program, memory, crystal energy or color as well as holy water or water from a sacred well. You can also add essences or herbal solutions to the cleansing bath but make sure they are in sufficient dilution to avoid staining the bowl. If you add essential oils, make sure that they have been emulsified first as essential oils used neat could leave an oily coating on the surface of the bowl as well as on the bath. You can do this by dissolving a few drops of essential oil into a tablespoon of vodka. Stir the mixture stating your intention and/or prayers as you go. Once your mixture has been made you are almost ready to immerse your bowl.

If you are using an enamel bath or hard container, place a clean towel in the bottom to prevent the bowl from being chipped. Immerse your bowl upside down in the bath (they are more stable this way). Soak the bowl overnight, or for however long feels right for you. Remove and place upside down on a towel or cloth to air dry. If you rub it with a towel fluff will stick to the granular surface of the bowl so air drying is preferable. Some people like to repeat this process once a year or at the solstices or other auspicious times. Once dry you can program your bowl with your chosen intention, see "programming" for further details.

Spring clean

The crystal bowls can get a little grubby as the granular surface of the bowl can hold on to dirt, especially if you work in the landscape as I do. Before you begin your spring clean ask that your positive intention and programming stays within the bowl and that any energy which no longer serves your purpose leaves and is transmuted into light.

Take your bowls outside if possible and put bottom up on a large tarp or plastic sheet. Hose them down or allow the rain to bathe. If you would like to make a cleansing solution you can put this into a misting bottle, one that is used to spritz indoor plants is perfect. Once the bowl is wet take some sea salt granules and a toothbrush and brush the salt over the surface of the bowl. This should remove most of the dirt but if you have stubborn or greasy marks you can use a natural soap or eco-friendly washing up liquid if that resonates with you. Hose down to remove any salt/soap residue and turn the bowls right side up. Fill them with a little water and sprinkle a small amount of salt and/or your personal cleansing solution into the bowl. Slosh the liquid around inside the bowl with your hand, reinforcing your intention as you do so. Allow the solution to sit for a while inside the bowl before emptying. Rinse with clean water and leave your bowl to air-dry.

In-between cleanse

In between each wholing session you can use mists, holy water, smudge or whatever you prefer to help transmute denser energy from the bowl. Some people feel the need to do this if they have had a release of negatively charged energy when working with the bowl.

Programming your bowls

As we have already explored, at a quantum level thought is a form of subtle energy and therefore any intention will add to the energy of your sessions. Quartz crystal has the ability to harness and transmit energy so is perfect for holding an intention or imprint of a sacred space.

In the *"Tantra of Sound"*, Jonathan Goldman states that the crystal bowls *"are marvellous at amplifying our intent on the sound"*. Just like regular crystal, crystal bowls can be programmed with your intentions which will be carried on the sound-wave when you play. Think about the program you would like for your bowl. It can be an overriding general program such as *"this bowl balances my energy on all levels"* or a specific program, for example *"this bowl is working with my heart chakra"*. When you have chosen your program sit holding your bowl, stating your intention out loud. State it in the present tense as though it is already doing what you ask rather than *"this bowl helps me relax"*, rather than *"this bowl will help me to relax"*. You may also like to place your intention on a piece of paper inside the bowl. Playing your bowl anti-clockwise (or clockwise if you are left handed) has the intention of bringing the energy towards you and into the bowl. State your intention and play the bowl anti-clockwise until you feel you have finished. You may like to repeat this process over a period of time. You can also use planetary hours, full moons, solstices and other potent times to reinforce your program or to add to the energy of your bowl. My bowls have been to many sacred sites including Stonehenge and Avebury in England and The Great Pyramid and The temple of Karnak in Egypt. They have been to the Arctic circle, to the dessert and to the sea as well as under planetary alignments, full moons, eclipses and solstices. Every time they are programmed with a new experience their energy grows!

Caring for your bowl

I wrap all of my bowls in blankets. You can buy carrying cases that are made for crystal bowls or you can buy drum cases. It depends on the size of your bowls and what you intend to do with them. If you are going to travel with them then you may need to give some thought to their transportation. When I fly with my whole set I pack mine into large aluminum trunks filled with packing material to absorb any in-flight bumps. You can stack two or three bowls inside each other for easy storage. Make sure each one is well wrapped before doing this as they can easily chip if they are knocked together. Sometimes my therapy room is set up ready to receive clients and therefore I will cover my bowls between sessions to prevent dust getting into them.

I prefer to place my tools on mats or throws rather than on the ground (unless I am working at a sacred site where I sometimes make an exception). I personally like to create a sacred space when I do any sound-work as it helps me to center myself and reinforce my intention. You can find some lovely throws, cushions and mats to place your bowls on. You may like to color code them depending on the chakra that the bowl is related to. It is so wonderful to see the bowls sitting on their throws ready to go to work. They almost gleam with the care that has been bestowed upon them by their loving owner.

Playing your crystal bowl

A crystal bowl is played by running a wand around the outside in the same way as you would play a Himalayan bowl. When you buy your bowl it will usually come with a rubber ring to sit it on and a wand to play it with. The wand will either be a suede covered stick or a wooden stick with a rubber ball end. A frosted bowl under 12 inches (approximately 30 centimeters) will usually play better with a suede wand and a bowl over 14 inches (approximately 36 centimeters) will usually play better with a rubber ball wand, but experiment with both. If you have a very large crystal bowl you may also like to buy a large soft mallet such as a gong beater for gentle donging of the bowl, which is lovely to do to announce your bowl at the beginning of a sounding session. A small clear bowl will play with a suede wand or one with a smaller, harder rubber ball on the end which you can buy from a music shop.

A good word to have in your head when playing the crystal bowls is "sensitivity". Long and low playing is more efficient at entraining the brainwave frequencies and facilitating an altered state.

Once you have set your space and stated your intention you may like to announce your bowl by tapping it lightly with the wand or soft beater one or more times before playing. When you are ready gently begin to run the wand around the top of the bowl until it reaches the desired volume and take the wand away, allowing the bowl to sing. You may hear gentle undulations and/or get the sense that the sound is going round and round the room. You may hear the sound in one ear and then the other which is the sound bouncing off the walls as well as balancing the right and left hemispheres of the brain. When the sound has decayed (which can take over a minute with some crystal bowls) begin to play the bowl again. Another technique is long and low playing which is the same technique that we covered in the section on Himalayan bowls. Begin playing the bowl until you have reached low to medium volume. When you have achieved this slow the wand down so that the bowl keeps singing at the same volume. You can play in this way for as long as you like.

Exercise: Getting to know your crystal bowl

Aim: The aim of this exercise is to introduce your crystal bowl to your energy system.

This exercise is the same as the one you did when you got to know your Himalayan bowl. Set your space and spend time meditating with your bowl without playing. Feel the energy of the crystal and get the sense of your energy blending with the energy of the bowl and vice versa. Do you get any images or feelings from the bowl and/or a sense of how it wants to be used? Announce your bowl by donging it gently at each of the four directions; north, east, south and west. Then begin to play softly in the "long and low" style. Spend time bathing in the sound and at the end of the session stop and let the silence flood in. Breathe and focus on your chakras and levels of being, checking for resonances in the system as usual.

Exercise: Sonic massage

Aim: The aim of this exercise is to work on any resonances that you have identified.

Begin playing the bowl. Feel the sound of the bowl on all levels of your being. If you have a bowl that is small enough to hold, move it slowly up and down the midline and within the auric field. It doesn't matter if your bowl is too big to hold as the sound will permeate your being at a cellular level anyway. Spend at least five minutes playing long and low and allow the sound to entrain your energy. Notice how this feels on all levels of your being.

Pause for several moments and breathe from the belly, checking in on the physical body and ask if there is anything your physical level needs from you. Begin playing again for another five minutes, carrying on this pattern of playing and breathing for as long as necessary and tuning in to your emotional level. Ask how you are feeling on this level and if there is anything that it needs from you right now. If anything comes up for you that is negatively charged breathe it out with a sigh on "AHH". You can always go back and work with anything that is still with you at the end of the session or refer to the enquiry methods in Part 1 for further investigation. Play for another five minutes, checking in with your mental level and asking if there is anything that this level needs from you. At the end of this exercise, spend several minutes in silence. Feel the sound in your being and tune in to your spiritual level without playing. How does this level feel? Write down how you felt during the session.

Make sure you are fully grounded before carrying on with your daily activities especially if they involve driving or operating machinery.

Exercise: Voice and crystal

Aim: The aim of this exercise is to feel the interaction of the voice with the crystal and to enhance your sounding session.

Begin by warming up your voice for a few minutes. Choose a crystal bowl with which you are able to sing comfortably. Play the bowl long and low, bringing your voice in at the same pitch when you are ready. Spend at least five minutes toning along at the same pitch with different vowel sounds. Then begin to bring overtones in at the same pitch and feel the difference. When you are ready use your intuition and tone and overtone in different pitches, allowing the voice and crystal to communicate with each other in a free and easy way. Write up any resonances that you have found at the end of the session if you want to keep a record. Make sure you are fully grounded at the end.

Exercise: Sounding with the mind of God

Aim: The aim of this exercise is to communicate with the universal sound and to allow you to be guided by the sonic signatures of your different tools.

Set your sacred space and place your Himalayan and crystal bowls in front of you. Begin by announcing all of your bowls in turn and listen to each bowl as it interacts with the other. There will be some bowls which sound harmonious and others which sound discordant. Both harmonious and discordant sounds can be beneficial so aim to use both in your session. Begin to play intuitively, bringing your voice in as and when it feels right. You can tone, overtone, and/or use "HU" or "OM". Match your voice to the crystal and Himalayan bowls for a few minutes to bond with them before exploring by using different pitches. Play slowly and simply as complicated and fast playing will shift your brainwaves out of a relaxed state. At the end thank your tools for joining with you in your sounding session, check in to the system as usual and make sure you are fully grounded.

"This new rhythm consciousness is oriented not toward performance and musical virtuosity, but toward personal transformation, consciousness expansion, and community building."

Anne Cushman

The Rhythm of Life

Since time began we have been governed and moved by rhythm. Rhythm is within us; it is surrounding us and we cannot live without it. From the sound of our heartbeat to the movement of the heavenly bodies we all move to the rhythm of life. Our first sonic experience would have been our mother's heartbeat and the whooshing of the blood rushing through her veins; perhaps this is why the gentle lub-dub of a heart-beat is so comforting. When you hear a prolonged drum beat you automatically entrain to its rhythm. You are also influenced by the tone of the drum and the harmonics contained within its song.

When you play a drum you make a connection with the sound of the drum as well as establish a relationship with the animal that helped the drum to be born. By playing a drum made from animal skin you are allowing the animal to live on through your rhythm. Drumming synchronizes the left and right hemispheres of the brain and balances the masculine/active and feminine/receptive energies within. Drumming improves the effectiveness of the immune system and reduces stress. Studies undertaken by renowned cancer expert Barry Bittman MD demonstrated that group drumming actually increases cancer-killing cells. According to Bittman, *"group drumming tunes our biology, orchestrates our immunity, and enables healing to begin."*

A drum is a membranophone which is an instrument that is played by beating a membrane which has been stretched over a frame. It consists of a body which is usually hollowed out and a taut striking surface. It was believed that the earliest drums were fallen tree trunks and there is also evidence that Australian Neolithic inhabitants played porous rocks which would have resonated when struck. Hand made drums have been discovered in almost every part of the world, the oldest being from around 6000 b.c.e. Drums have been found in Mesopotamian ruins and Egyptian tombs and there are several caves in Peru which have wall markings indicating that drums were used in various aspects of life. Due to their consciousness altering ability drums were often featured in ritual and ceremony. American Indians used wood and gourd drums for their rituals, celebrations and music. In Africa drums were used to communicate over a distance.

The pitch can be changed by tightening and loosening the membrane which is achieved by heating and cooling the skin or by tightening it with ropes or cord. You can also get frame drums with adjustable frames, allowing you to change the pitch by changing the diameter of the frame and therefore tightening or loosening the skin. In many parts of the world drums were (and still are) venerated, and believed to contain a spirit or entity.

Drums and gender

A frame drum has a diameter that is greater than its depth and has long been associated with healing, journeying and transformation. The frame drum appears in many cultures all over the world including North American, Lapland, Siberia, North Africa, Greece, Tibet, Turkey and Italy. There are single and double-sided frame drums, the most common being single sided. Sometimes the frame drum is also called a "hand drum" or "shaman's drum". Some cultures consider the frame drum to be more feminine in energy, perhaps for its moonlike appearance. Djembe's, Conga's, Bougarabou's and other drums of this type (where their depth is greater than their diameter) are considered in some cultures to be more masculine in energy, again probably because of their shape.

Some cultures have strong beliefs about who should and shouldn't play the drums, and which type of drums women and

Male and Female Drums

men should play. There are documents that state Sami women were not even allowed to touch the frame drum although the Sami people I have spoken to say that this was very rare and possibly was confined to one or two groups across Lapland. In Finnish Lapland the shaman traditionally played the frame drum, but this was probably due to there being more shaman than shamanka's at that time. When Christianity swept through Scandinavia and into Lapland many of the shaman's drums were broken or burnt and the shaman pressurized into converting to Christianity. With the attention on the men the women quietly preserved the traditions and kept the spirit of the drum and Joik (a type of chanting or singing) alive. Today the drum culture is very strong among the Sami women.

There is a reference to young boys and women of the Asabano in Papua New Guinea being forbidden to play drums in case they become sexually aroused. According to Roger Lohmann, author of *"Sound of a Woman: Drums, Gender and Myth among the Asabano of Papua New Guinea"* the Asabano feel that *"playing the drum is to have sex on a mythological-symbolic level."* Playing drums in a certain way can stimulate the base and sacral chakras so perhaps the Asabano felt the need to control the energy flow in this area. Interestingly, the church tried to put a stop to this practice saying that it *"belongs to a Satanic past"* and in 2005 both men and women drummed together during a Baptist church service to symbolize unity. Outside of the church, however, drumming remains a male activity.

In her book *"When the Drummers Were Women"*, Layne Redmond states that *"sacred drumming was part of a woman's skills which were used as a powerful tool for communal bonding and individual transformation until the fall of the Roman Empire"*. There are many historical references to both women and men playing the frame drum. As energy is gender neutral, I believe it is personal preference that dictates which kind of drum you prefer to play as well as the reason why you are playing it. I always use a frame drum for wholing work and ceremony and occasionally play my Bougarabou or Djembe when I am performing with my group "Soundscapes".

Single sided drums

You can get some very good artificial skin drums. Remo have a good range of synthetic skin drums which sound great and are very handy if you are intending to play outdoors as they will not be affected by the weather and air temperature. I love to play at sacred sites and if I am conducting a ceremony or performing outside I always take my trusted synthetic skin drum with me. Animal skins will be sensitive to room temperature and weather which can be a disadvantage if you are working outdoors. If the skin gets wet it will sag; warm or hot skins tighten and ring with a higher tone when struck and you may lose some of the deeper tones.

In my opinion there is something very special about working with the energy of an animal. In shamanic traditions animal (and sometimes human) parts were used to make sacred instruments as it honored the animal or human and allowed them to live on after death. I appreciate that this does not resonate with everyone and it is important that you find what feels right for you.

If you are buying a drum made from the skin of an animal, do your best to find out as much as you can about the animal, whether it was killed or died of natural causes and if every part of the animal was used. If your supplier is unable to answer your questions or you are not happy with what you are told you may prefer to look elsewhere or make your own drum. If you love a drum and are unsure of its history you can always conduct your own ceremony to honor the animal when you get home. The following list of animal properties may help when choosing a drum, or you may prefer to wait for a drum to choose you. You may find one comes onto your path if you send out the message that you are looking.

Cow & Bull

The cow is associated with the moon, fertility, nourishment and giving. The bull is associated with the sun, the Earth, strength and fertility. It may not always be possible to find out the gender of the animal skin that may have been used to make your drum so I would not worry too much about this aspect. The energy of the cow and/or bull brings productivity, strength, patience, security and sensitivity to your drum. If you need to embrace any of these qualities then perhaps a cow or bull skin drum is for you.

Buffalo

The buffalo brings grounding and stability together with abundance. When head and heart are aligned anything is possible and the buffalo helps you to connect with both of these levels of being to help you to manifest your hearts desire. If you require balance and grounding to bring your dreams in to reality then perhaps the buffalo is for you.

175

Deer/Reindeer

The deer has a vibration of gentleness, innocence, strength and spirituality. The branches of a stag's antlers are seen as antenna stretching into other dimensions which is one of the reasons why the deer is seen to have a spiritual connection. The antlers are also associated with the tree of life which is a symbol of harmony and creation. The fruit from the tree of life represents different stages of spiritual growth.

Goat

The goat is steadfast and sure-footed so if you require balance you may wish to bring some goat energy into your life. If you require stamina and energy to achieve a long-term goal the goat will help you get there. The goat is also a symbol of fertility and abundance and being a mountain animal it has associations with the higher self.

Horse

The horse is associated with finding freedom, travelling to new places and being able to see the path ahead. The horse also has associations with clairvoyance and personal power. If you are feeling constrained the rhythm of the horse may help you to see a way to be free. Horses are also associated with the wind and the foaming waves of the sea, so if you have a horse-skin drum take it to the seashore on a windy day and gallop together on the rhythm of your drum!

Making your own drum

If you have never made a drum before I thoroughly recommend making your own sacred drum. It is a wonderful experience and one that can bond you to your transformational tool for life. If this is something that you would like to do, do your research and find a good workshop that honors the animal, the rhythm and your process.

Double sided drums

Double sided drums are found in many cultures, the most popular being in Tibet and America. The two sides are approximately 3 to 4 inches apart which means that when one side of the drum is struck the other side will also start to ring creating harmonics. According to the Jade Wah'oo *"the double-sided drum enables us to communicate in the sacred language of spirit".*

Drums Being Made During a Drum Therapy Workshop

A double sided drum is very special to use for drum journeys, shamanic work and ceremony but can be rather heavy if you are holding it for a long period of time. The handles of Tibetan shaman drums are usually ornately carved with symbols and deities. Between the skins is placed a cowry shell representing the sacred feminine and a stone from a sacred site. These produce a lovely percussive ringing sound when the drum is struck. A genuine Tibetan shaman's drum is a considered purchase but well worth it if you are intending to do drum journeying and/or ceremonial work. Be aware that there are cheaper versions on the market that are not the genuine article so

A Tibetan Double Sided Shaman's Drum

if you intend to buy a Tibetan shaman's drum, check your sources carefully. A genuine drum may look very old, as though it has been cobbled together over many years (which it probably has!). The frame can be warped and it is likely to have a dark mahogany colored skin. It may also smell of smoke due to the times it has been heated over the fire. These drums are usually played with a curved stick. Traditionally a Tibetan shaman's drum will be passed from shaman to student, but as the young people are choosing to move to the cities and with Tibet undergoing a lot of changes there are fewer students that want to study the shamanic traditions. If there is no student to pass the drum to it would usually be destroyed when the shaman died. However some people feel that it is important that the drum continues the work and so some drums are now finding their way to the West.

Care of your drum

We know that animal skins are sensitive to temperature and therefore you need to consider this when storing and playing your drum. If your drum is too slack put it in a warm place for a few minutes and the skin will tighten but take care not to over tighten the skin by putting it somewhere too hot or the skin could split or get so tight that it buckles the frame. Do not play outside in the rain or put water on the skin unless you know what you are doing as this could cause it to slacken too much, resulting in the drum needing to be re-skinned. I speak from experience!

I was holding a workshop where we were working with the energy of sacred sites and this particular weekend the water element had made itself present rather a lot! We had been to Stonehenge where we had been lightly to moderately rained upon for an hour. We were working with the voice and the Peruvian Whistling Vessels so this was not a problem, in fact the rain added to the atmosphere. The following day we were working inside during the day and at Avebury stone circle in the afternoon. During the day there was occasional drizzle but on the whole the skies looked as though they were clearing. In the afternoon we prepared for our final session inside Avebury and gathered our instruments of choice which were drums, didgeridoos and singing bowls. We headed for the stones under a cloudy but dry sky. As we began to set the space the rain started, first as a fine drizzle closely followed by a downpour! We did our best to shelter our drums under our jackets and continue playing, but in the end we gave in and saw the humor of the situation. We were too far from shelter so we all got soaking wet! I now have three drums which need to be re-strung but I look back on that day very fondly. It was possibly the wettest but the most fun Sonic Alignment workshop I have ever done!

I like to keep my drums in bags or wrapped up in fleeces when I am not using them as this protects the skin. There are plenty of padded drum bags on the market or you can make your own if you prefer. If you are buying or making a drum bag it is ideal if it has an extra pocket on the side for your drum beaters. If you can't get a drum bag with a pocket you can wrap your beaters in a cloth and put them inside the hollowed out section of the drum but make sure they don't rest against the outer side of the skin as they could stretch or even pierce the skin if there are any sharp edges on the beater.

Different drum beaters will make different sounds against the skin of the drum. The harder beaters will allow the higher sounds to ring out, the softer beaters make a softer, bass sound against the skin. Depending on the tension of the skin you will get different sounds from the drum and beater so you may wish to experiment with different beaters when you are playing the drum in different temperatures. You will also find that your drum has "sweet spots" on its surface where the sound really sings out and where different harmonics can be heard.

Exercise: Getting to know your drum

Aim: The aim of this exercise is to familiarize yourself with the energy of this wonderful tool for wholing and transformation.

Spend time holding and examining your drum. Feel the skin, tune in to the drum before playing it. If it is made from animal skin and you know what animal it is made from you may like to honor the animal and ask for its properties to live on through your rhythm. You may like to create your own ceremony to honor its life. You can still do this if you are not sure which animal your drum skin is and you may find you get the answer during this session.

Begin playing the drum. Move your beater all around the skin and listen for changes. Change your rhythm and see if there is a particular one that you and your drum enjoy. Then switch off your mental level as much as you can, step out of the way and allow the rhythm to wash over you for at least five minutes. At the end of your session stop, breathe and check for resonances on all levels of being.

What rhythm are you in?

There are times when life takes on a gentle, easy and meandering rhythm and other times when life seems to move very fast. The different rhythms of life have an overall effect on our health and wellbeing and also have an impact on our life. How many times have you got out of bed in a hurry, stubbed your toe, tripped over the cat, knocked into the door and known that you had a bad day ahead? Could this be because you have "set" the energy rhythm for the day on some level?

Different states of being have different rhythm signatures which manifest in the form of thoughts, feelings, events, symptoms and dis-eases. I believe that we have an overall rhythm signature, just like we have an overall fundamental tone. To discover the rhythm you are in try the following exercise.

Exercise: Finding your rhythm

Aim: The aim of this exercise is to identify your fundamental rhythm.

You may prefer to make sure you are on your own for this exercise as some people feel a little self-conscious when they first experiment with rhythm in the body. March around like a soldier and feel the two-beat rhythm in your body. Really get into the one-two-one-two pacing of this rhythm and feel it on all levels of being as your energy interacts with the feeling of this rhythm. How does it feel? People often come up with words like *"active"*, *"logical"*, *"dynamic"*, *"strong"*, *"matter of fact"*, *"faster"* and even *"aggressive"* to describe this rhythm.

Now try a waltzing, one-two-three rhythm. Really feel this in the body as you move around the room. Some say that this three-beat rhythm is *"receptive"*, *"softer"*, *"musical"*, *"peaceful"*, *"joyful"* and *"flowing"*.

As with everything in life we require a balance of both rhythms states to be in optimum health but you may find you have a tendency towards one rhythm over another. Ask yourself which rhythm you felt most comfortable with. Did you resonate with one rhythm more than the other? Is there one that you are "in" most of the day? Is the rhythm you are in the same as the one you resonated with, or is it different? If it is different do you feel that this is having an adverse effect on you? What effect do you feel that being in this rhythm is having on your levels of being?

It is important to remember that there is no right or wrong or better or worse; they are just different. It is how you feel that counts. Once you begin to notice which rhythm you are predominantly in, you can begin to work with rhythm for wholing and transformation.

Exercise: Rhythm identification

Aim: Identifying the predominant rhythm states in your life helps you to achieve balance on all levels of being.

Make two columns on a page. In one column put a list of the tasks and activities that you do in a day and in the next column write which rhythm you think that each task is in. For example,

Task/Activity	Rhythm
School Run	Two-beat
Journey to and from work	Two-beat
Work	Two-beat
Relationships	Two-beat
Swimming	Three-beat
Massage	Three-beat

Looking at the above example you can see that this person considers the above activities as being mostly two-beat.

You can break each activity down further by noting any rhythm changes within the activity or task. Take work as an example.

Task/Activity	Rhythm
Work AM	Two-beat
Lunch	Three-beat
Work PM	Two-beat

This person's work is predominantly a two-beat activity for them. Once you have identified your rhythm you can treat yourself by using a "rhythm vitamin" in the form of a counter-rhythm to balance your energy using the entrainment principle. Over time, the use of rhythm-vitamins will help to realign the system on all levels.

You can go even further by noticing the tempo of your life rhythm as well as the beat. Is your life a drudging two-beat stomp or a fast-paced two-beat rhythm that would reduce the most hardened techno music enthusiast to tears? If it is the former, try giving yourself a boost with a faster two-beat rhythm for a while before introducing a softer three-beat rhythm or a composite rhythm (I'll cover these shortly). If it is the latter I suggest a composite rhythm followed by a gentle three-beat rhythm vitamin and a serious lifestyle change before you implode! Seriously though, if you are running a fast-paced two-beat rhythm for a long period of time you need to find a way to balance this.

Rhythm therapy

You don't always need a drum to give yourself a little rhythm therapy. If you need a quick fix when you are at work or in a stressful situation you can tap out a rhythm on your leg or a table or clap your hands if you are without your drum, or you can count it out in your head if you prefer, it works really well. Having said that there is no substitute for working with the beautiful reassuring sound of a drum.

The drum is a very important part of my sound therapy kit and it has produced some amazing results with my clients, some of whom have been suffering from long-term and even chronic dis-ease. If the rhythm of your life is out of alignment with your true rhythm it stands to reason that long-term exposure could cause imbalance in the system. One could say that in the West we are predominantly in a fast two-time rhythm. Two-time rhythm without any three-time rhythm will entrain the system into running a faster pattern which over time can lead to stress on the adrenals, heart and other systems of the body. I believe this fast rhythm causes anxiety and other stress related illnesses as well as mental fatigue, ME and burnout. It is very similar to your brain being in high Beta without Alpha, which we know results in stress, anxiety and exhaustion.

Exercise: Rhythm vitamins

Aim: The aim of this exercise is to treat yourself with a counter rhythm to bring balance to the system.

Start off by beating your predominant life rhythm for a minute or so and then slowly bring the rhythm vitamin in, spending at least five minutes entraining the system to this rhythm.

Predominant life rhythm	Rhythm vitamin
Two-time	three-time
Three-time	two-time

Don't be surprised if you find your rhythm vitamin challenging at first. The longer your system has been entrained to one rhythm, the more resistant you may be to the rhythm vitamin because it is contra to your programming. Do your best to stay with your counter-rhythm and check in with your levels of being during and after the exercise. Even if you are resisting on one level, you may find that your rhythm vitamin is feeding you on others. Aim to do this exercise as often as you can, ideally once a day for a week or two. As your inner rhythm changes, so your outer world will change so look out for any self-sabotage techniques that you may put in your way (remember Harry the Hermit crab? Don't slip back into that old shell). You may like to combine the drum with voice or Himalayan bowls to help your system process what comes up for you during your sounding sessions.

Rhythm caffeine

If you need a quick pep-me up in the morning or you want to prepare yourself for something that requires mental application try a short burst of a fast paced two-beat rhythm to give yourself a boost. People naturally pace around when they need an energy boost or need to "think on their feet". If you have several drums, choose a higher pitched drum as this will also stimulate energy flow or you can heat your drum slightly so that the skin tightens or use a harder beater to bring out the higher tones.

Rhythm hot chocolate

If you need to relax the system, choose a drum with a lower tone or use a softer beater and spend a few minutes beating out the "lub-dub" rhythm of a heart beat. If you can, match it to a resting pulse of around 60 beats per minute. After a few minutes you should feel calm and relaxed.

Composite rhythms

Composite rhythms are a balance of both rhythm types and therefore could be seen as being neutral. They are very useful to use as a bridge between your current life rhythm and where you feel you need to be. For example if you are running a very fast-paced two-beat rhythm you may be too resistant to a slow undulating three-beat rhythm but you *know* that's what you need. In this case you can use a composite rhythm to help slow you down and you will find that after a few minutes in this rhythm your system accepts the slow three-beat rhythm much more easily.

Think "American Indian" for this rhythm (although traditionally the rhythm used by American Indians is a three-beat with the emphasis on the first beat, but this was changed when the first cowboy films came onto our screens). This rhythm is a faster two-beat rhythm with the emphasis on the first beat, *one*-two-three-four and so on. This rhythm is really useful if you require stimulation but do not want the adrenaline to start pumping too much. It is also quite joyful and is great to use with groups, especially when you are also using your voice.

Drum journey

This technique has long been used by Shaman and Shamanka's to align to the mind of God and bring back guidance and teachings from other realms. It is believed that the drum was the most popular instrument for journeying because of the unique properties it has to enable a person to be grounded and yet at the same time the beats entrain the brainwaves to be in frequencies that facilitate a shift in consciousness. The harmonics created by the beats also carry the player and listeners to other realms.

Exercise: Drum journey

Aim: To sound the mind of God through the spirit of the drum.

When you feel ready make sure you won't be interrupted for at least half and hour. Set your space in whichever way you prefer and use the lightest drum and beater that you own as your arm may get tired if you're not used to drumming in this way.

Begin by breathing from the belly. When you are ready start beating the drum with a lub-dub heart rhythm for a minute or two to settle you in, speeding up slowly to approximately four or five beats per second. Stay there for at least twenty minutes if you can (you may need to work your way up to this length of time). Keep your shoulder relaxed and your arm and wrist flexible as it will help you to drum for longer. Keep the tempo even but you may find the drum takes over and that a few accents and variations in the rhythm pop in. There may be a point where you begin to lose awareness of your physical body and align to the mind of God. Voices, other sounds, images and colors may come into your mind. All of this is part of your experience and is there for you to learn from. If at any time you feel uncomfortable you can either stop or you can breathe and play through it. When you feel you are ready to bring your session to a close stop on a beat without slowing down and allow the silence to flood in. Stay in the silence for a few minutes, feeling the sound in the body and checking for resonances as usual.

If you feel ungrounded, spend time coming back, take a drink and use the grounding methods that you prefer (see the section on grounding).

Ocean Drum

Ocean drums are so called because that they make a sound like the ocean. They are made all over the world, but more commonly in the USA, Nepal, India and Bali. Some have Buddhist symbols on them and some have Sanskrit syllables, mantras, mandalas or other decorations. They are double sided and contain ball-bearings, pebbles or seeds which run backwards and forwards as the drum is rocked. The ball-bearings also have a massaging action on the reflex points of the hands. To play this drum, balance it on the palms of the hands gently tipping the drum to the left, right and round in a circular motion. Sitting with an ocean drum for a few minutes will relax the most stressed of people!

You can also use your drum as a percussion tool by gently beating it with a soft drum beater. The balls inside the drum jump and make a crunching sound when played which adds a new quality to a percussion group or grounding session.

"That which is Below corresponds to that which is Above, and that which is Above corresponds to that which is Below in the accomplishment of the Miracle of the One Thing."
Hermes

Planet Earth Calling - Grounding

As above so below. To expand your energy effectively and with a lasting effect you need to remain centered and grounded. When you are centered, grounded and fully present in the moment you are able to reach for the stars, ask for the Moon, and get it! As you work towards en-lightenment your energy expands into a new and larger energy box which can result in feeling light-headed and removed from reality. After a while your system will adjust but in the meantime you still need to function in the physical world .

Some of the exercises in this book may produce powerful effects and therefore it is a very good idea to make appropriate space and time in your life before immersing yourself in your sounding sessions. It is not advisable to undertake one of the deeper sound exercises just before a business meeting or the school run! In my experience sound has an accumulative effect and therefore the more you work with sound the easier and faster your energy will expand as you open yourself to another level of potential. You will also get used to the feeling of being "phased out" but however experienced you become it is important that you make sure you are fully grounded, especially if you are about to drive or operate machinery.

It takes only a few minutes to ground your energy. You don't necessarily need any instruments for this but shakers, rainsticks, ocean drums, claves and rattles are all good grounding tools. If you are using rainsticks and ocean drums, shake them like a rattle. If you use gentle soothing sounds you will slip back in to an altered state. Drums do the same thing, so avoid using a drum as a grounding tool. If you don't have any grounding instruments simple stamping and clapping will work just as well. You can also make your own shakers by using old mineral water bottles (the small ones are better) filled with rice, crystals or small pebbles.

When you have finished your session, take a rattle and shake around the auric field and chakras making a sound like a rattle-snake. You can do this by shaking the rattle rapidly back and forth as if you were fanning yourself very fast. Pay attention to any particular chakras or parts of the body that you were working on during your session. If you are clapping, clap vigorously around the body and over the chakras you were working on. Once you have finished, begin to make your grounding more rhythmic in a slow two-beat rhythm. Stand up and stamp along to the beat getting progressively faster and faster. Stop when you are ready and take in the silence. Have a drink, visit the loo and have something light to eat as all of these physical activities are very grounding.

"Many people find it difficult to believe that a state of consciousness totally free of all negativity is possible. And yet this is the liberated state to which all spiritual teachings point. It is the promise of salvation, not in an illusory figure but right here and now"
Eckhart Tolle

Full Circle

Together we have explored our outer and inner realms. We have looked at how the mind of God is sound and that we are connected to this wonderful source of all that is. Through our sounding sessions and self-awareness exercises we can improve our health and wellbeing and enable a deep and profound communication to take place. We have worked with many techniques and have come full circle by grounding our energy in the moment.

There is a saying that *"the only gift is the present"* and this is true. The only way we can really influence the past or future is in the moment. By remaining in the moment we are able to fully realize how we are resonating with the world. Eckhart Tolle, author of *"The Power of Now"*, states that *"all forms of fear are caused by too much future and not enough presence"*. Anxiety and fear are indications that your mental level is spending too much time in the future dwelling on the "what ifs". He goes on to say that *"all forms of non-forgiveness are caused by too much past and not enough presence"*. Guilt, regret and resentment are indications that your mental level spends too much time in the past. We would not want to release our memories completely as these are part of us but if the echoes of the past hold you in an unhealthy state of being in the present, by being aware of the resonances as they manifest in the moment and transmuting the imbalance we are able to expand our energy field and transcend to an infinite number of possible futures. Anything and everything is possible!

This book has been quite a journey during which my greatest challenge was deciding what to leave out! It was really important for me not just to share my work (and the work of other's that I have also featured) but to allow the work to live through simple exercises. The words on the page only truly come to life when they are put into practice. I hope that by working with the exercises in this book you have to identified and transmuted energy imbalances and holding patterns, as well as formed a lasting relationship with therapeutic sound. It is my intention that this book will be one of many and if this is the case, I hope to work with you again soon!

Sonic Blessings
Lyz Cooper

An Invitation

If you have enjoyed this book and would like to take your sound-work further Lyz runs talks and workshops all over the UK and overseas and has developed several professional sound therapy training courses.

For further details, dates and other information, please see her website www.healthysound.com or contact us, details below.

Soundworks and The British Academy of Sound Therapy
PO Box 1111
Chichester
West Sussex
PO19 9HP
England
Tel 00 44 (0) 1243 544454
mail@healthysound.com
www.healthysound.com

Sources

Books

Aburrow, Y (2000) *The Magical Lore of Animals,* Capall Bann Publishing

Andrews, T (1999) *Animal Speak,* Llewellyn Publications

Ashley-Farrand, T (2000) *The Healing Power of Mantras,* Gateway

Becker, R.O and Selden, G (1985) *The Body Electric,* Quill

Berendt, J E (1988) *The Third Ear, Listening to the World,* Element

Brodie, R (2000) *The Healing Tones of Crystal Bowls,* Aroma Art Limited

Buzan, T (2003) *The Mind Map Book,* BBC

Cope, J (2004) *How to Khoomei,* Wild Wind & Sound for Health

Cousto, H (2000) *The Cosmic Octave,* LifeRhythm

Cytowic, R (1993) *The Man Who Tasted Shapes,* Puttnam

D'Angelo, J (2001), *Healing with the Voice,* Thorsons

Dyer, W (2004) *The Power of Intention,* Hay House

Emoto, M (2004) *The Hidden Messages in Water,* Beyond Words Publishing

Farhi, D (1996) *The Breathing Book,* Owl Books, Henry Holt and Company

Godwin, J (1991) *The Mystery of the Seven Vowels,* Phanes

Galgut, P (2005) *Humming Your Way to Health and Happiness,* O books UK and USA

Goldman, J (1992) *Healing Sounds,* Element Books

Goldman, J (2005) *The Tantra of Sound,* Hampton Roads

Goleman, D. Boyatzis, R & Mckee, A (2002) *The New Leaders,* Time Warner

Goswami, A (2001) *Physics of the Soul,* Hampton Roads Publishing Company Inc.

Goswami, A (1995) *The Self Aware Universe,* Tarcher Penguin

Greene, B (2004) *Fabric of the Cosmos,* Penguin Books.

Hesse, H (1946) *The Glass Bead Game,* Vintage

Hoyle, F (1983) *The Intelligent Universe*, Michael Joseph Limited

Inayat Khan, H (1991) *The Mysticism of Sound and Music*, Shambhala Publications, Inc.

James, J (1993) *The Music of the Spheres*, Abacus

Jansen, E, R (2002) *Singing Bowls*, Binkey Kok Publications

Jasmuheen (1995) *In Resonance*, Koha Publishing, (Germany), Self Empowerment Academy (Australia)

Judith, A (2004) *Eastern Body, Western Mind*, Celestial Arts

Judith, A (1987) *Wheels of Life*, Llwellyn's New Age

Kaku, M (2005) *Parallel Worlds*, Penguin

Katie, B (2002) *Loving What Is*, Harmony Books

Keyes, L.E (1973) *Toning*, DeVorss and Company

Leeds, J (2001) *The Power of Sound*, Healing Arts Press

Lindahl, K (2003) *The Sacred Art of Listening*, Sky Light Paths Publishing.

Lipton, B, H (2005) *The Biology of Belief*, Mountain of Love

Lohmann, R, I (2007) *Sound of a Woman: Drums, Gender and Myth among the Asabano of Papua New Guinea*. Cited http://ingenta-connect.com/content/berg/mar/2007

McTaggart, L (2001) *The Field*, Harper Collins

Motoyama, H (1981) *Theories of the Chakras*, Quest

Myss, C (1996) *The Anatomy of Spirit*, Bantam

Pearce, S. (2005)The Alchemy of the Voice, Hodder and Stoughton

Pert, C (1997) *Molecules of Emotion, Simon and Schuster(UK), Scribner(USA)*

Redmond, L (1993) *When Drummers Were Women*, Three Rivers Press

Ross & Wilson (2002) *Anatomy & Physiology*, Churchill Livingtone

Sacks, O (2007) *Musicophilia*, Picador

Samanta-Laughton, M (2006) *Punk Science*, O Books

Simpson, L (1999) *The Book of Chakra Healing*, Gaia

Swami Atmananda (2002) *Chakras & Nadis*, New Dawn

Swami Sivananda Radha (2005) *Mantras, Words of Power*, Timeless Books

The Collins English Dictionary (1986) William Collins Sons & Co Ltd

The Holy Bible, King James Version, Oxford University Press

Tiwari, Bri. Maya (2000) *The Path of Practise, The Ayurvedic Book of Healing with Food, Breath and Sound*, Motilal Banarsidass Publishers Private Limited

Tolle, Eckhart (1999) *The Power of Now*, New World Library (USA) 2001, Hodder and Stoughton (UK)

Wah'oo, J (1992) *Nature of Shamanic Doctoring*, Shamanic News, March 1992, p.3.

Werbeck-Svardstrom, V (2002) *Uncovering the Voice – The Cleansing Power of Song*, Sophia Books

Wolf, F.A (2002) *Matter into Feeling.* Moment Point Press

Articles and Journals

Bittman, B et.al (2001) Composite effects of group drumming music therapy on modulation of neuroendocrine-immune parameters in normal subjects. Published Alternative Therapies (2001) Vol.7.1

Hawkes, N (2003) *The Lowest Sound in the Universe*, Sunday Times September 11th

Inayat Khan, H (2002) Parsi Anfas, Gatha 1

Films

Happy Feet (2006) Warner Brothers

Lord of the Wind Films (2005) *What the Bleep do we Know?* Revolver Entertainment

Byrne, R (2006) *The Secret*, TS Productions LLC

Spielberg, S (1975) *Jaws* Universal Pictures

Lucas, G (1997) *Star Wars*, Lucas Film Ltd

Websites

www.bbc.co.uk/1/hi/england/1829053.stm

http://www.bethcoleman.net/gamma.html

www.businessballs.com/kolblearningstyles.htm

http://cosmicaromatherapy.tripod.com/chakrahealing2.html

http://www.deepermind.com/maslow.htm

http://www.doctorbrainwave.com/what_are_brain_waves.htm

www.frankperry.co.uk

www.glcoherence.org

www.healingsounds.com

www.jillpurce.com

http://www.sciam.com/article.cfm?id=regrowing-human-limbs

www.sheldrake.org/papers/Morphic/morphic_intro.html

www.telegraph.co.uk

www.thesecret.tv

www.thework.com

www.timesonline.co.uk/tol/news/world/article1157687.ece

www.tree.org/b1d.htm

http://en.wikipedia.org/wiki/Akashic_records

http://en.wikipedia.org/wiki/Fraunhofer_line

BOOKS

O is a symbol of the world, of oneness and unity. In different cultures it also means the "eye," symbolizing knowledge and insight. We aim to publish books that are accessible, constructive and that challenge accepted opinion, both that of academia and the "moral majority."

Our books are available in all good English language bookstores worldwide. If you don't see the book on the shelves ask the bookstore to order it for you, quoting the ISBN number and title. Alternatively you can order online (all major online retail sites carry our titles) or contact the distributor in the relevant country, listed on the copyright page.

See our website www.o-books.net for a full list of over 500 titles, growing by 100 a year.

And tune in to myspiritradio.com for our book review radio show, hosted by June-Elleni Laine, where you can listen to the authors discussing their books.